George Washington Holley

Magnetism

It's Potency and Action

George Washington Holley

Magnetism

It's Potency and Action

ISBN/EAN: 9783743370661

Manufactured in Europe, USA, Canada, Australia, Japa

Cover: Foto ©Thomas Meinert / pixelio.de

Manufactured and distributed by brebook publishing software (www.brebook.com)

George Washington Holley

Magnetism

MAGNETISM

ITS

POTENCY AND ACTION

WITH SUGGESTIONS FOR A NEW

COSMOGRAPHY

AND A NEW

CELESTIAL GEOGRAPHY

BY GEORGE W. HOLLEY
AUTHOR OF "NIAGARA, ITS HISTORY AND GEOLOGY."

BOSTON:
ARENA PUBLISHING COMPANY
COPLEY SQUARE
1894

Copyrighted, 1894,
By GEORGE W. HOLLEY.

All rights reserved.

PREFACE.

FOR many years the writer of the following pages has been much interested in, given much thought to, and made sundry notes on the subjects of which they treat. Not, however, until his removal to Ithaca, in 1882, where he could avail himself of the facilities for further study and experiment afforded by Cornell University, has he been able to make a systematic attempt to formulate his ideas and conclusions.

Still he has been obliged to quote some authorities at second hand, while some he wished to consult he could not procure. He has also been obliged to omit some experiments he would have been glad to perform. A slight fire in his room partially destroyed some of his notes, the result of which is that some passages appear in quotation marks for which his memory does not enable him to quote the authorities.

The reader will observe that much consideration has been given to the subject of magnetism, a form of energy whose universal action, the various and numerous ways in which it is manifested, the subtle influences which it exerts and exhibits in different conditions have not, as the writer believes, been accorded the importance they deserve. Except in its most striking manifestations in connection with electricity—electro-magnetism—and in animal magnetism it has not been fully investigated. In its finer and more subtle form as manifested in animal and vegetable life, especially in the minutest bodies, it seems to have been still less studied. Those forms of energy, the universality, pervasiveness and constancy of their action, it is one object of the writer to set forth and demonstrate. The same form of energy that swings the stars in their well-ordered courses forever wings the flight of the tiniest moth that perishes in a day.

The facts and observations concerning the influences that prompt the action of animals, kine, dogs, birds and insects, the multifarious forms and conditions of animal and vegetable life, and the persistence of the life force are chiefly new so far as shown by the authorities we have consulted in the excellent reference libraries of Cornell University and Columbia College. The field is wide and fertile and we have entered into details that would be irrelevant except that they elucidate the varied forms of magnetic energy.

Some of our readers may prefer to consider electricity rather than magnetism to be the most efficient of the natural forces. We have given our reasons for preferring the latter. Our views concerning magnetism will be held to be entirely untenable by those who believe it to be "only electricity in rotation" and that electricity is not a "form of energy." After the writer had finished his notes on the properties of magnetism he saw for the first time Dr. Hodge's "Modern Electricity" and was gratified to find that some of his (the writer's) views and suggestions are fortified by so acute a thinker and so vigorous a writer. He was also gratified to note the just tribute offered by Dr. Hodge to the memory of the late Prof. Joseph Henry, the first discoverer of Telegraphy.

If the writer has seemed to express himself with undue earnestness and confidence in some portions of his work, he begs the reader to believe that it has been in no spirit of dogmatism. Further observations and experiments with improved instruments and under favorable conditions may tend to prove the truth of our main hypothesis. If we have presented any new truth, or any new fact or suggestion of permanent value that may help other students to take other onward and upward steps in this sublime field of investigation, we shall be satisfied. The labor has been one of ever increasing love, admiration, and adoration.

ITHACA, N. Y., July 18th, 1891.

Explanation.

The reader will note that the author, in treating of "matter" in several portions of the work, has described it in different terms, not contradictory but disconnected. Instead of rearranging them in order to present a more condensed and logical conclusion, he decided to leave them, with this explanation, as they were copied from his original notes.

Errata,

which the reader will please correct before reading the book.

Page 7, second line from bottom, read "widest" for "wildest."
Page 65, first line, read "an" for "and."
Page 69, sixth line from top, between the words "beings" and "that" insert the words "permits us to suppose."
Page 72, attach asterisks (*) to the numerals IV, I, II, III.
Page 89, at end of first paragraph, omit the quotation marks.
Page 128, twelfth line from top, read "rhythmic" for "rhythmatic."
Page 171, second line from top, read "pairs" for "pair."
Page 183, seventh line from top, read "a" for "the."
Page 201, seventeenth line from top, read "intense" for "immense."
Page 224, third line in first stanza of poem, read "starry" for "stony."
Page 226, third line in ninth stanza, read "upbore" for "implore."
Page 277, the first two lines of the last paragraph should read as follows:
"The hyperbolas that revolve about their principal axes generate a hyperboloid of two nappes."

MAGNETISM.

I.

Subject Proposed.—Object to be Attained.

SINCE Sir Isaac Newton's announcement and exposition of the laws of gravitation, so called, and their application to all matter, but more especially to the stars and planets and all other celestial bodies, no other subject, probably, has so fully occupied and exercised the minds of investigators of natural phenomena. This is especially true in regard to the stellar systems, and what may be called the Geography of the Heavens. The profound and intensely interesting investigations of Swedenborg, the Herschels, Laplace, Kant, Struve, Father Secchi and others, large as is the store of knowledge they have supplied, still leave much to be learned.

The facts concerning the stars, suns, planets, nebulæ and other celestial bodies considered as things, as material bodies moving in space, their elements, motions, periods, their mass, volume and weight, their relations to and influence on each other, have been more or less fully and satisfactorily ascertained and described. But the *system* under which the whole mass, the grand aggregation of the celestial bodies is arranged, their common centre, if they have one, their present and future positions, the probable or possible changes to which they may be subjected and the probable or possible periods of their existence, are still undetermined.

The object of this memoir is to consider the present state of our knowledge on the subject, to glance at the different theories of the stellar cosmography, and then, after classifying and collating such truths and facts as observation—which is a mental act,—experiment—which is a physical one,—and experience—which is the knowledge gained by experiment—have supplied us, to consider what further progress may be possible in our explorations of this most extensive and sublimest field of human knowledge.

From Prof. Newcomb's lucid and admirable work "Popular Astronomy" we quote a striking paragraph which will more fully suggest the range and scope of our design. It is as follows: "The widest question which the study of the stars presents to us may be approached in this way: We have seen in our system of sun, planets, and satellites, a very orderly and beautiful structure, every body being kept in its own orbit through endless revolutions by a constant balancing of gravitating and centrifugal forces. Do the millions of suns and clusters scattered through space and brought into view by the telescope, constitute a greater system of equally orderly structures ? and if so, what is that structure ? If we measure the importance of a question, not by its relations to our interests and our welfare, but by the intrinsic greatness of the subject to which it relates, then we must regard this question as one of the noblest with which the human mind has ever been occupied. In piercing the mystery of the solar system, and showing that the earth on which we dwell was only one of the smaller of eight planets which move around the sun, we made a great step in the way of enlarging our ideas of the immensity of creation and of the comparative insignificance of our sublunary interests. But when, on extending our view, we find our sun to be but one out of unnumbered millions, we see that our whole system is but an insignificant part of creation, and that we have an immensely greater fabric to study. When we have bound all the stars, nebulæ and clusters which our telescopes reveal into a single system, and shown in what manner each stands related to all the others, we shall have solved the problem of the material universe considered, not in its details but in its wildest scope."

While most profoundly impressed with the

magnitude of our task we may say, varying and extending slightly the phrase of Bacon, that "if we shall succeed in effecting anything to the purpose, what led us to it was a true and genuine humiliation of mind" and a sincere desire to somewhat enlarge the boundaries of human knowledge and manifest forth the Divine Glory.

II.

Space, Matter and Time.

BEFORE considering the stellar systems and more particularly the planetary system of which our sun is the centre, it will be profitable to consider some preliminary and most important questions which stand in direct and most intimate relation to the whole subject. They relate to Space, Matter and Time. It is not proposed to consider the abstruse metaphysical nor the elaborate physical definitions of these elements, but merely to define them in the simplest terms that will enable the general reader to understand their value. While we have many speculations and suggestions concerning them, we have no succinct, comprehensive and satisfactory definition of either. Still we know their functions, their uses, and distinguishing characteristics. Space is the medium which contains all Matter and in which all forces are developed and manifested. It can be bounded only by itself, and, since any limit whatever must be contained within another limit, it follows inevitably that it has no limit.

Matter is an accretion, larger or smaller, of atoms or molecules that exist in a gaseous, liquid or solid state. It cannot exist without Space. It can have no extension or motion without Time. The swing of a pendulum records a second of time; it also passes, simultaneously, through a second of arc in space, and by friction at the pivot of the pendulum-rod a molecule of matter is dissipated.

Matter may fill all space, or, in isolated portions, it may fill different parts of space. It may exist under an infinite variety of conditions and forms, and consequently may be changed, transformed and transmuted, but can never be destroyed. It *may* have an infinite number of deaths, it *must* have an equal number of resurrections.

It is interesting to note one of the earliest expressions of this idea of the indestructibility of matter. Marcus Aurelius in Meditation V. 13, writes: "I am composed of the formal and the material; and neither of them will perish into non-existence, as neither of them came into existence out of non-existence. Every part of me then will be reduced by change into some part of the universe, and that again will change into another part of the universe, and so on forever." Again, in Med. VI. 15, "Some things are hurrying into existence and others are hurrying out of it; and of that that is coming into existence part is already extinguished. Motions and changes are forever renewing the world, just as the uninterrupted course of time is always renewing the infinite duration of ages."

Again, in Med. IX. 28, " Soon will the earth cover all: then the earth too will change, and the things also which result from change will continue to change forever, and these again forever."

Time is the element—Bacon and Kant called time and space " forms"—which marks the growth, development, continuance, change or decay of all things and of all forms and conditions of life, organic or inorganic. In particulars it is limited; in the concrete it is limitless. Strato of Lampsacus wished time to be called the " measure of movement and rest." Aristotle called it the " measure of duration." Newton would make " duration another name for absolute time." Condensing these suggestions we may say that Time is the measure of motion and rest. The motion of a point in space generates a line; the motion of a line in the direction of its greatest dimension generates a plane; the motion of a plane in the direction of its greatest dimension generates a solid.

The infinitesimal quantity of space is a point; the same quantity of matter is an atom or a molecule; the same quantity of time is an instant. If we could conceive of the beginning of all things and at the same time imagine the existence at once and together, of a point in space, an atom of matter and an instant of time, then the addition of another atom of matter would require the addition of another point in space, and to make this addition would consume another instant of time. By the continuous and perpetual repetition of this process we should make an infinite accretion of the different constituents. Thus in this trinity we have the germ of a physical universe, and in it we also observe the direct, intimate and perpetual union of Space, Matter and Time, their perfect and absolute correlation. In and by and through them we become acquainted with the somatology of matter and all the forms, varieties, properties and uses of force or energy.

III.

The Stellar and Planetary Systems.

In studying the stellar and planetary systems the first objects to demand our attention are the stars themselves, including both suns and planets; and after these, asteroids, nebulæ, comets and meteorites. It is not proposed to enter into any historical details concerning them. We know, as already stated, their position, their composition, their characteristics and the laws which govern their motions. Of the medium, space, that they occupy and in which all their motions are executed; of the force or forces which insure their stability; of the manner in which those forces act; of the system and order in which they are arranged and distributed in space; concerning all these we have much to learn. It is proposed to collect and collate such facts and theories as bear upon these points, and then to determine whether, from strict analogy and legitimate deduction, we are not entitled to advance still farther from the known into the unknown.

"I am," says Faraday,* " exceedingly adverse

* Conservation of Force.

to the easy and unconsidered admission of one supposition upon another, suggested as they often are by any imperfect induction from a small number of facts, or by a very imperfect observation of the facts themselves; but, on the other hand, I think the philosopher may be bold in his application of principles which have been developed by close inquiry, have stood through much investigation, and continually increase in force."

IV.

Force and Motion.

LET us now turn our attention to force and motion. The chief forces of nature, so called, are magnetism, electricity, heat, light, chemical affinity and gravitation. From these, singly or in combination, all motion is derived, what are called the " mechanical powers " not, of course, being considered. Since the general acceptation by physicists of the validity and efficacy of what Grove calls the " correlation," Faraday the " conservation " and Herbert Spencer the " persistence " of force, all meaning the same thing, the law which Faraday characterizes as " the highest in physical science which our faculties permit us to perceive," the progress of physical science has been unprecedented in extent and never exceeded in importance. In the long and earnest endeavor to establish the principle of the correlation of forces some physicists entertained the idea, amounting almost to a conviction, that it might ultimately be proven that there is, if not an absolute unification of all physical forces, which are differentiated only by variation of conditions, at least a single force which should permeate all others, and connection with which should be indispensable for their efficiency. Says Faraday * (§ 2146), "I have long held an opinion amounting to conviction, in common I believe with many other lovers of natural knowledge, that the various forms under which the forces of matter are made manifest have one common origin, or, in other words, are so directly related and mutually dependent that they are, as it were, convertible into one another and possess equivalents of power in their action. Again, farther on, he says (§ 2702), "The long and constant persuasion that all the forces of nature are mutually dependent, having one common origin, or rather being different manifestations of one fundamental power, has made me often think of the possibility of establishing by experiment a connection between gravity and electricity, and so introducing the former into the group, the chain of which, including also magnetism, chemical force and heat, binds together so many and such varied exhibitions of force by common relations."

"All the non-magnetic metals," he says (§ 2295), " are subject to the magnetic power," and further after the discovery of diamagnetism he says (§ 2420), that "all matter appears to be subject to the magnetic force as universally as it is to the gravitating, the electric and the chemical or cohesive

* Experimental Researches in Magnetism.

forces ;" also (§ 3174), " that whatever idea we employ to represent the (magnetic) power ought ultimately to include electric forces, for the two are so related that one expression ought to serve for both.

Magnetic and electric lines of force are analogous, and considering the existence of these lines of force he says (§ 3273), " *The magnet is evidently the sustaining power.* In every point of view, therefore, the magnet deserves the utmost exertions of the philosopher for the development of its nature both as *magnet* and a *source* of *electricity.*" Such are the opinions of this distinguished philosopher. They are more or less fully corroborated by many others. One of his most distinguished contemporaries, the late Prof. Maxwell, commenting upon his experiments in magnetism in its relation to the ether and the electro-magnetic rotation of light says (Address before the London Institution), " The vast planetary and inter-stellar regions will no longer be regarded as waste places in the universe which the Creator has not seen fit to fill with the symbols of the manifold order of His kingdom. We shall find them to be already full of this wonderful medium; so full that no human power can remove it from the smallest portion of space or produce the slightest flaw in its infinite continuity. It extends unbroken from star to star; and when a molecule of hydrogen vibrates in the Dog-star the medium receives the impulses of these vibrations." Of similar purport is the following extract from Sir W. Thomson's Papers on electrostatics and magnetism: "It is often asked, are we to fall back on facts and phenomena and give up all idea of penetrating that mystery which hangs around the ultimate nature of matter? . . . It does seem that the marvellous train of discovery, unparalleled in the history of experimental science, which the last years of the world have seen to emanate from experiments, must lead to a stage of knowledge in which laws of organic nature will be understood in this sense: that *one* will be known as essentially connected *with all*, and in which unity of plan through an inexhaustibly varied execution will be recognized as a universally manifested result of creative wisdom." More emphatically accordant with the foregoing views are those expressed by Helmholtz in his "Aim and Progress of Physical Science": "It has actually been established as the result of investigations, that all the forces of nature are measurable by the same mechanical standard, and that all pure motive forces are, as regards performance of work, equivalent." . . . . "Whether the foregoing considerations chiefly seek to elucidate the logical value of the law of conservation of forces, its actual signification in the general conception of the processes of nature is expressed in the grand connection which it establishes between the entire processes of the universe through all distances of place or time. The universe appears, according to this law, to be endowed with a store of energy which, through all the varied changes in natural processes, can neither be increased nor diminished; which is maintained therein in ever-varying phases but, like matter itself, is from eternity to eternity of unchanging magnitude."

Says Grove in "concluding remarks" on the "Correlation of Physical Forces": "The conviction that the so-called imponderables are modes of motion, will, at all events, lead the observer of natural phenomena to look for changes in these affections, whenever the intimate structure of matter is changed; and conversely to seek for changes in matter, either temporary or permanent, whenever it is affected by these forces. . . . It is a great assistance in such investigations to be intimately convinced that no physical phenomena can stand alone; each is inevitably connected with anterior changes, and as inevitably productive of consequential changes, each with the other, and all with time and space; and either in tracing back these antecedents or following up their consequents, many new phenomena will be discovered, and many existing phenomena, hitherto believed distinct, will be connected and explained. Explanation is, indeed, only relation to something more familiar, not more known, *i. e.*, known as to causative or creative agencies.

"In all phenomena the more closely they are

investigated, the more we are convinced that, humanly speaking, neither matter nor force can be created or annihilated, and that an essential cause is unattainable. Causation is the will, creation the act, of God." "The natural philosophy of the future," says Tyndall (Heat as Motion, p. 351), "will certainly, for the most part, consist in the investigation of the relations subsisting between the ordinary matter of the universe and the wonderful ether in which this matter is immersed." These citations are sufficient to indicate the current of scientific opinion on the point above referred to, and also to convince us that there is an earnest, abiding hope and conviction that grand results are yet to be attained by further faithful work in this direction.

In this chapter we have preserved the nomenclature of the distinguished scientists whom we have quoted, in order that we might show the change that has taken place in that nomenclature, by giving the terminology finally adopted by modern scientists. The terms "correlation," "conservation," and "persistence" of force are no longer used. It is now settled that *energy*, to which we have referred in the sequel, is the thing conserved, and forces are factors of energy, of which there are different kinds or varieties exhibited under different and varying conditions. Of the unity of what are called the "forces of nature" all physicists are practically convinced, but what term shall define that unity is not settled. The unity consists in reducing them all to modes of motion of which there is an almost infinite variety, many of which we have set forth in the sequel.

V.

Magnetism and Electricity.

WE propose now to set forth in detail the more important results of observation and experiment which have been reached up to the present time, results of truths and facts in the grand curriculum of physical science which furnish the material for both the foundation and the superstructure of a new Cosmography and a new system of Celestial Geography. Let us begin with magnetism and electricity. To the strong, earnest, reverent genius of Faraday, science is indebted for the most original, extended, subtle and lucid expositions of the properties, characteristics and effects of magnetism considered as a force, and also of those of electricity, though less fully. After finishing his famous experiments in which he succeeded in rotating a ray of polarized light by magnetic and electric forces he says:* "Thus is established, I think for the first time, a true, direct relation and dependence between light and the magnetic and electric forces, and thus a great addition made to the facts and considerations which

* Exp. Res. in Magnetism, Vol. III. pp. 19-20.

tend to prove that all natural forces are tied together and have one common origin."

" A magnet placed in the best vacuum we can conceive acts as well upon a needle as if it were surrounded by air, water or glass, and therefore these lines exist in such a vacuum as well as where there is matter." * " All magnets first originate lines of magnetic force which other magnets under one condition will receive and conduct, and, under another condition resist and repel, exhibiting the ordinary conditions of magnetic attraction and repulsion. But currents of electricity are competent to produce or induce collateral currents, and magnets are proved competent to produce like currents, thus showing the identity of action of magnets and currents, in producing effects different from those of ordinary magnetic attractions and repulsions. External to the magnet, those concentrations which are named poles may be considered as connected by what are called magnetic curves or lines of magnetic force, and which exist in the space around." " These phrases have a high meaning, and represent the ideality of magnetism. They imply not merely the directions of force which are made manifest by the smallest magnet, but also those lines of power which connect and sustain the magnetic polarities and which exist as much when there is no magnetic needle to show their presence as when there is."

* Exp. Res. in Magnetism, p. 415.

The earth, according to Gauss, is a great magnet whose power is expressed by the utterly incomprehensible sum of eight octillions of pounds. "Experiments prove that there is no loss, or destruction, or evanescence, or latent state of magnetic power, caused by distance, nor in consequence of the convergence or divergence of the lines of force or obliquity of their intersection." (§§ 3110, 3112, 3113.) "Such an action (Magnetism, § 3075) may be a function of the ether, for it is not at all unlikely, if there be an ether, it should have other uses than simply the conveyance of radiations." "It may be a vibration (§ 3263) of the hypothetical ether, or a state of tension of that ether equivalent to either a dynamic or static condition."

"A magnet presents a system of forces perfect in itself, and able, therefore, to exist by its own mutual relations." Let us especially note that there is *no other force* of which this can be said. "It has a dual and antithetic character belonging to both static and dynamic electricity, as is demonstrated by the opposite powers of like kind formed at its poles. These poles are related to each other not only through or within the magnet itself, but also by external curves or lines of force, without which they cannot exist," * since it is impossible to construct a magnet with a single pole. "Though the physical lines of force of a magnet

* Exp. Res., Vol. III., p. 441.

must be considered as extending to an infinite distance around it, so long as it is isolated, yet they may be *condensed, compressed* into a very small local space by other systems of magnetic power."

From ordinary magnetism, Faraday (Vol. I., §157) developed electricity, and refers (Vol. III., p. 524) to Carnot's experiment with a revolving disk, in which he found currents of electricity competent to produce collateral currents and magnets proved competent to produce like currents. And notwithstanding the generally accepted impression that all metals lose their magnetism when raised to a red heat, he declares that the magnetic metals retain a certain amount of magnetic power, whatever their temperature.

Arago discovered the fact that when a copper plate or disk is rotated below a freely suspended magnet, the latter tends to follow the motion of the plate. This is the effect of a magnetic force pure and simple. And Faraday explains it as arising from electrical currents induced by the magnets in the rotating disk, thus proving, in this case at least, that the action of magnetism and electricity are identical. He also states (§ 2514) that "if a copper disk suspended by a long string is set whirling, and is then introduced into the field of an electro-magnet, its motion will be instantly arrested, and it cannot be further rotated in the field." In this case, also, it is the magnetic force that proves effective.

Again, Helmholtz * writes, a copper disk set in a wood frame, with multiplying gear, and rotated with great rapidity, was placed between two pieces of iron which did not touch it, being part of the armor of an electro-magnet. Turn the current of a 3-cell battery round this magnet, and the pieces of iron act like a break that entirely stops the rotation of the disk, and it can only be started again by the application of a strong force. Here, also, the result is due to magnetism, or the magnetic force. Prof. Tait, also, a conservative and accomplished physicist, notes † that "where a conducting body is made to move in the neighborhood of a magnet, the relative motion of the two produces currents of electricity in the conductors. If a copper disk be kept so moving, the faster it moves the stronger the currents become, until, finally, the disk is heated and melted;" thus proving that intense heat is evolved from magnetism alone, there being no friction of surfaces. This is in conformity with Oersted's investigations, which linked together magnetism and electricity, and also with Ampère's conclusion, that all the properties of a permanent magnet can be explained on the hypothesis of electrical currents circulating in a fixed direction around the magnet. If two polished disks of zinc and copper be brought into close proximity and kept there for some time, and either of

* Phil. Mag., 1867.
† Recent Advances in Physical Science.

them has irregularities upon its surface, a superficial outline of them will be traced by each upon the other, showing the action of *magnetic* force. If the disks be connected with a delicate electroscope, and then suddenly separated, the electroscope is affected, showing that superficial radiation from surface to surface has produced *electrical* force.*

"All substances conduct electricity in some degree." † "There are no bodies," says Daniel, ‡ "which are absolutely non-conductors; all conduct electricity more or less slowly. There are no bodies that are perfect conductors; all offer more or less resistance to the flow of electricity."

One of the most important and comprehensive actions of magnetism is that manifested in chemic force. Its wide range of affinities and activities is marvellous; its various combinations and mixtures are infinite in number. Every stomach, every apparatus for secretion and digestion in every living organism is a chemical laboratory in constant operation. Every vegetable growth, from the least to the greatest, is a product of chemic force. The earth is one vast laboratory for the production of germs, roots, stems, cells and protoplasm for every possible variety and form of plant-life. It energizes all living matter and reproduces new life from death and decay. Its most amazing ex-

* Grove, Con. of Forces, p. 58.
† Ganot's Physics, p. 566.
‡ Principles of Physics, p. 527.

hibition is its selective faculty. The vast fertile portions of the earth are covered with innumerable forms and varieties of vegetation, of every shape and color, producing every variety of fruit to gratify the taste and of flowers to charm the eye.

Plant organisms of different size, form, function, and color grow side by side in the same soil, the same atmosphere and under the same conditions. The fruits and flowers that they produce are as various in flavor and in fragrance as they are almost infinite in number.

To the electro-chemic force we are indebted for all forms of crystallization—for gems and precious stones, for the agates and malachites, for the numerous variegated marbles, and, especially, for the lodestone, without which ocean navigation would be nearly paralyzed by day and entirely so on starless nights.

We have in the sequel (p. 33) noted the fact that the greatest magnetic tensity in different bodies is manifested at their edges and pointed ends. In cylindrical bodies or any bodies with curved surfaces it is distributed more or less uniformly through the exterior surface. In trees, shrubs and plants the character of the organism as to density, elasticity, color, graining, etc., is determined by the electrical and chemical action of the nutritive material with which, through the aid of light, heat and moisture the organism is built up. Müller found that the electrical action in growing trees and shrubs was most effective in the extremities of the roots and branches, thus confirming Darwin's observation, as to the roots, that their irritability—sensitive growth—was localized in their tips. This also corresponds with the action of magnetism in solids.

The dynamic energy of magnetism is very strikingly shown in the growth of shrubs, plants and trees. All these except air-plants derive their nourishment from the earth and the air.

One of the most conspicuous exhibitions of atmospheric magnetism, if we may so designate it, is seen in the growth of trees standing in groves in an open country. All the branches of the trees growing on the edges of the grove are strongly drawn outward by the magnetism in the atmosphere and in the unshaded earth, while the inward growth, towards the shaded earth and shadows of the trees, is exceedingly limited, except near and at the tops which are fully exposed to the light on all sides so that the branches stretch out equally in all directions. This characteristic of tree-growth is especially exhibited in trees that stand isolated in open fields. They present broad, beautiful, bushy tops, and attain a larger growth than the same class of trees standing in forests.

Young trees of any kind, but especially fruit trees standing on either side of a thick grove, will be stunted in growth, and after reaching a certain height the branches will be drawn toward the light and in due time will be so curved as to stand nearly at right angles with the bole. No branches will grow towards the grove. Light, the magnetic force that compels all these branches to grow in one direction, is as efficient as any mechanical force could be, though slower in action.

One of the most beautiful exhibitions of tree-growth is the *graining* of the wood. The word is not found in the best text-books in botany, and the fact is only slightly indicated in the description of the *stratified* growth of the organism. The principal elements in building up the organism are the roots and stems, the former drawing from the earth the substantial ingredients that furnish the protoplasm of the stem with its branches and leaves.

The nutriment of different kinds utilized in tree-growth is stored in cells. These cells are of different form and size and are disposed in different positions in the tree trunks and branches. Some of them stand upright, nearly parallel to the axis of the stem. But much the larger number of them stand at different angles with the axis, as may be seen when they are strongly magnified. Each cell has its own wall, and as the tree advances in age their composition is changed. When the cells are small, thin, short and narrow and lie parallel with the trunk-axis, the grain of the tree will be straight, fine and uniform. When the cells are longer and broader with thicker and more porous walls and when they are disposed at different angles with the axis of the trunk then the fibrous stratification is more manifest and the curved, wavy and forked lines and veins of the grain are more fully developed. In some species of trees the cells are variolate, presenting an appearance similar to the pittings of small pox; others are verticulate, disposed in sworls. These two classes of cells are strongly developed in the curl and spotted maple, the graining of which is often very beautiful. In all trees the laminated structure that forms the rings which mark the annual circumferential growth of the tree is most rapidly developed while the tree is young. The width of the rings is always greatest next to the centre of the stem and they grow narrower each succeeding year.

We have seen the butt of a white oak the annular rings of which proved it to be more than four hundred years old, and after being sawed some axe-marks near its centre were shown to have been made more than one hundred and fifteen years before Columbus discovered America.

That the density and strength of the cell walls is greater than that of their contents may be demonstrated by applying an acid of proper strength to the clean surface of the heart-wood of any tree. The contents of the cells will be eaten out and the cell walls will appear like a collection of small pits, as indicated below. If these be rubbed hard with a bit of polished steel a smoother and harder surface will be made than can be made in any other way.

The rapidity of growth and graining of the tree varies with the season. In the spring, after the winter's rest and after the rain showers have thoroughly moistened the earth and the rays of the sun have become more ardent, then the roots are most active and the growth of the tree is most rapid. And the graining is then also most rapidly developed, being aided by strong winds and gales which sway and bend the stem in all directions, resembling what would be the action of a wet cylindrical sponge when bent, in forcing the moisture to the surface of the inner curve. There is also absorption of what Sachs calls the "nutrient fluid" from without. Thus the growth progresses rapidly until the autumn when the leaves fall and the sap descends through the roots to the earth. Then follow the colder months of the autumn and winter. During this period the bole and branches undergo a hardening process, making the wood more dense, tough and strong. In tropical climates they are hardened by heat, by baking as it were. To this high temperature also, is due the gigantic vegetable growths of those climates.

Says Sachs, * " Chemical processes in the interior of the growing body is always connected with these (micellæ) processes of growth. The nutrient fluid which penetrates from without contains in fact the

* Text Book of Botany, pp. 666–7.

material for the formation of micellæ of a definite chemical nature; but the material is chemically different from the micellæ which it produces. Thus starch grains are nourished by a fluid which clearly does not contain any starch in secretion, and again the cell wall grows by the absorption of substances out of the protoplasm which are not dissolved cellulose. .... Growth by intussusception is therefore connected not only with a continual disturbance of the molecular equilibrium, but also with chemical processes in the interior of the growing structure. Chemical compounds of the most various kinds meet between the micellæ of an organized body so that they act upon and decompose one another. It is certain that all growth continues only so long as the growing parts of the cell are exposed to the atmospheric air. The oxygen of the air has a decomposing effect on the chemical compounds contained in the organized structure; with every act of growth carbon dioxide is produced and evolved. The equilibrium of the chemical forces is also continually disturbed by the necessary production of heat and this may also be accompanied by electrical action. The movement of the atoms and molecules within a growing organized body represent a certain amount of work, and the equivalent forces are set free by chemical changes. The essence of organization and of life lies in this: that organized structures are capable of a constant internal change, and that so long as they are in contact with water and with any oxygenated air only a portion of their forces remains in equilibrium even in their interior, and determines the form and framework of the whole, while new forces are constantly being set free by chemical changes between and in the molecules, which forces in their turn occasion further changes. This depends essentially on the peculiarity of micellar structure, which permits dissolved and gaseous (absorbed) substances to penetrate from without into every point of the interior and to be again conveyed outwards." From this extract we learn that in all growing plants the moisture of the atmosphere exercises an important function. It acts like a balance wheel in an engine; it secures uniformity of action, of energy, and this secures uniformity of growth. The atmosphere is never entirely free from moisture as was abundantly demonstrated by Tyndall. To this fact is due the abundant juiciness of tropical and semi-tropical fruits, melons, oranges, pineapples, etc., that grow on light soils with infrequent rains.

Says Grey,* "The color in trees is owing to special vegetable products, or sometimes to alterations resulting from age." Chemical action and electricity, as noted above, also exert an influence. This is true as to single, separate trees. But why trees of different species growing in the same soil, the same climate and the same atmosphere should

* Text Book of Botany, Sec. 147.

differ entirely in grain and color, one being of a pure white like the outer layers of rough-bark hickory, another the dark shade of the black oak, another with the deep red of the mahogany, another with the soft, bright yellow of satin wood, we do not know. Through some subtle alchemy of nature the roots and sap seem to be endowed with a selective faculty that enables them to supply the particular protoplasm necessary for each variation of wood, form and color. This selective faculty must be mainly due to chemical affinity and combination. There are also various nutrient vegetables grown beneath the earth's surface. There are others that are rank poisons. All these are indebted to the selective faculty of the roots, especially to what the old botanists called the nib, for their distinctive characteristics. It is the chemic force that dyes the foliage of tree, shrub and flowers, that paints the neck of the dove and the breast of the robin. The red rose and blue violet are as red and as blue at midnight as at mid-day. Light is the subtle and potent alchemist that reveals them to our consciousness.

VI.

Electricity ; Magnetism ; Vacua ; Radiant Heat ; The Universal Force.

IN some experiments made by Mr. John Hopkinson, quoted by Sir Wm. Thomson,* he found that the *electric* current traversed with difficulty a partial vacuum, and that the more perfect the vacuum became the more effectually the current was impeded, until, in a vacuum as perfect as it is possible to create by artificial means, *the current was entirely checked.* M. Plücker employed Geissler a skilful glassblower of Bonn, to make permanently exhausted tubes for experiments in electric discharges in vacuo. In his experiments Plücker found that the luminous strata developed by these discharges and also the streams and glows after the discharges, obeyed magnetical influences in a remarkable way. Here we are reminded of the Aurora and the Zodiacal light, and still farther by the fact that, in one case—the discharge between two aluminium balls,—the striæ nearest the negative ball were

* Proceedings of Royal Society, Dec. 11, 1862.

truncated and of a pale *green* color, the color observed in those lights through the spectroscope, as we shall see in the sequel.

These discharges were also studied by Gassiot by means of a galvanic battery and other forms of electric generators. We also learn from Ganot * concerning Geissler's tubes that, "at the moment of being closed these tubes are exhausted and before sealing them a small quantity of gas or vapor and potash is introduced, so that its pressure does not exceed half a millimetre." Hence they were not perfect vacua. "When a tube three inches long and one inch in diameter, provided with very thin platinum electrodes five-eighths of an inch apart, was employed *no discharge passed* till the potash which it contained was *heated*, when a faint luminosity appeared, and immediately afterwards one and then two cloud-like striæ came from the positive wire, while round the negative a large brilliant glow was produced; as the discharge continued the negative wire became red-hot." In this experiment proof is obtained that the discharge will *not pass* in a very *perfect vacuum*, the presence of a certain amount of *matter* being *indispensable*, and then *heat* is developed. Of course the "heated" potash supplied the "matter" which destroyed the vacuum and was "indispensable" before the discharge could pass. Faraday demonstrated that the *magnetic* force freely traversed the same kind of vacuum, also

* Ganot's Physics, p. 723, Atkinson's Translation.

that similar *electrical* currents placed side by side add their quantities together and similar *magnetic* lines of force do the same, hence electric lines of force are analogous to magnetic lines of force (§§ 268, 269).

As indicating the *compressibility* of magnetism —a term repeatedly employed by him and other scientists—is the fact that a helix-carrying current can develop in an iron core a magnetic force of a hundred fold greater power than that possessed by itself (§ 3273). "All bodies are affected by helices as by magnets, and according to laws which show that the *causes* of the action are *identical* as well as the effects" (§ 22369), thus confirming the correctness of the opinion of Ampère as to the identity of the action of helices and magnets.

We also know that when the plane or square ends of a bar magnet are made conical or pointed their intensity and power are much increased. And we are led still further in the same direction by the experiments of M. Plantè who constructed some powerful secondary batteries by connecting the secondary elements side by side or in series. By thus connecting four or five elements and discharging them through a short, thick iron wire, he heated it to what may be called the boiling point, the centre of it being fused into a ball with bubbles of gas bursting from the interior. He also found that the secondary currents would magnetize electro-magnets much more powerfully than the primary currents from which they were derived. The maximum magnetization which a steel bar can acquire depends not only on the nature of the steel and its mode of tempering, but also on the dimensions of the bar. It is greater as the bar has the form of a longer and thinner cylinder. By working *very thin rods* Kohlrauch observed that the magnetic moment of steel may attain 100 units per gramme, which would give a strength of magnetization . . . nearly 10,000 times that of the earth.* Joule proved that bars of iron, nickel and cobalt were lengthened by magnetization and that when the action of the field is suppressed the bars shorten without returning to their original length. The elongation of cobalt is nearly twice that of iron.†

The blacksmith would find it necessary to apply many sturdy blows of his sledge hammer in order to elongate a bar of cold iron; but here is a silent, invisible, irresistible force that accomplishes this work, in a longer time, perhaps, but with equal efficiency. It is also proved that a bar of soft iron becomes heated when subjected to successive magnetizations and demagnetizations or to magnetizations in opposite directions.‡ The elongations by heat and the shortening by frost of iron

* Marcart and Joubert: Elect. and Mag., translated by E. Atkinson.
† Joule's Scientific Papers, Vol. I., pp. 235–264.
‡ Grove: Art. VI. Magnetism.

rails and other bars of iron exposed to the alternations of the weather are familiar facts. Prof. Crookes, by means of what he calls radiant matter, operating in vacuum tubes or bulbs of glass, produced the shadow of an aluminium cross on the phosphorized end, so to speak, of a bulb. The radiant matter thus projected not only made the glass phosphorescent, but also *warmed* it, a very remarkable result, indicating that if the strength of the induction coil were increased and its action longer continued the temperature of the glass would have been raised even, perhaps, to the melting-point.*

The mechanical action of this radiant heat is shown by the glass railway bulb, within which, on a pair of glass rails, a small wheel with wide mica spokes is propelled. This mechanical action is further exhibited in the beautiful electrical radiometer which carries within the bulb a fly—as Crookes calls it—with four square vanes of mica supported on aluminium arms, having beneath a ring of fine platinum wire, the ends of which pass through the glass and may be connected with an induction coil. On this being so attached as to make the platinum wire the negative pole the vanes were rotated with great velocity. Now as Faraday and Hopkinson demonstrated that electricity cannot freely traverse a vacuum, it follows that these and all similar results obtained by means

Gorton : Electricity and Mag., pp. 121, 122.

of these tubes must have been produced by magnetism or a magnetic force, since it has also been demonstrated that magnetism easily traverses a vacuum. Further, in regard to vacua we may note that Morgan, quoted by Grove,—Art. Light —"found no conduction by a good Torricellean vacuum," and that Masson found that the barometric vacuum does not conduct a current of electricity, or even a discharge, unless the tension is sufficient to detach particles from the electrodes;" and further that Gassiot " by adopting a plan of Dr. Andrews, viz.: absorbing carbonic acid by potash, succeeded in forming vacua across which the powerful discharge from the Rhumkorf coil will not pass." The old Realists—so called— spake more wisely than they knew when they declared that "Nature abhors a vacuum." This is sufficiently demonstrated by the fierce alacrity with which it hastens to fill one that has been produced by the operation of its own laws. When a vacuum is created in the air by the explosion of a thunderbolt the vast pressure of the whole terrestrial atmosphere instantly rushes in to fill it. Now, if it be true, according to the abundant evidence we have cited, that electricity cannot traverse a vacuum, it must be particularly noted that there can be no electricity in the medium or force that fills that vacuum, for all the electricity in the vicinity had been exhausted by the discharge of the bolt, and even if electric currents could have been present they would been ineffective. But magnetic currents or lines of force freely traverse a vacuum, and these must have supplied the force which restored the atmospheric equilibrium.

Leibnitz says, "The ultimate source of all motion is the *original force* lying in *all* bodies which may be restricted or limited in various ways by the conflict or collision of other bodies. *This force lies in all substances and a certain action always arises from it.*" This was written nearly 200 years ago, and is a very good description of the magnetic force as we know it to-day. Kant claims that Leibnitz founded the dynamic conception of nature which has since continued to prevail. The following may be accepted as a free translation of a significant passage in his (Leibnitz's) doctrine of Monads: "Matter must be always the same, since the monads are always the same; and force can never be destroyed since the monad can never be destroyed. The whole interchange of forces is simply the result of a greater or less degree of movement on the part of the *universal force* which every atom possesses, and all forces are, therefore, correlated with each other through motion." "And," continues Kant, "if the student of nature at the present day, in all his experiments and inferences, starts from and returns to this idea, if in all the varying phenomena and manifold magic of the outer world, his endeavor is always to grasp *the one natural force* and bring it into subjection to

THE UNIVERSAL FORCE. 43

thought and law, this mode of viewing things traces its origin to Leibnitz." And in summing up the doctrine of Leibnitz he argues that it was based " partly upon errors and partly upon truths," both of which he specifies. Among the truths is his express belief in " the animation of all things ; the recognition of an inner, active principle co-operating or rather operating in everything which stirs or moves."*

Magnetism may be imparted to different metals and other substances by slight contact, by friction, by induction and by impact, gentle or smart raps.

The latter method was suggested by Sir Isaac Newton when one of his contemporaries informed him that he could not succeed in repeating Sir Isaac's experiment of magnetizing by friction with a magnet, small bits of paper under glass, the two being slightly separated from each other. He informed his correspondent that if after duly applying friction, the paper did not rise to the magnet, he would gently rap the glass he would succeed, as he did. In this direction, after successfully repeating Sir Isaac's experiment, we further tested the method in the following manner, using flat-headed, soft, bright iron French nails, three inches long, $\frac{1}{8}$ inch in diameter, a lodestone hammer weighing four ounces and a small pocket compass. Making a rest for the nails in a bit of wood we treated them as follows, the head of each being

* Kant : Crit. of Pure Reason, pp. 279, 299.

presented to the positive pole of the needle immediately after contact.

Wire No. 1 slight contact for ½ second deflected the needle 34°
 "   " 2   "   "   " 2 seconds "   "   44°
 "   " 3   one light rap   "   "   30°
 "   " 4   one smart rap   "   "   38°
 "   " 5   ten   "   "   "   "   55°

We have used these facts, as will be noted in the sequel, when treating of hunting dogs.

VII.
Light, Heat and Magnetism; Chemical Action; All Natural Forces Equivalent.

WE know that light and heat are easily developed from artificial magnets. " Heat," says Bacon,* "is an expansive motion whereby a body strives to dilate and stretch itself to a larger sphere or dimension than it had previously occupied. Cold contracts or narrows most substances so that in intense frosts nails fall out from walls and brass cracks." Few residents of New England seventy years ago can have failed to hear, on a bitter cold morning, the sudden, sharp report that followed the starting of some of the wrought-iron nails that were used at that time in the erection of wood buildings.

When a bar of soft iron is held in the hand in a temperature of 60° F. no inconvenience is felt whether the hand be dry or moist, but let the iron be exposed in the open air over night when the temperature is 30° F. below zero, if it then be touched with a moist finger, it cannot be removed without abrading the flesh. A small horse-shoe

* Novum Organum, App. XX.

magnet, as was proved by the writer, had its magnetic power very materially increased by outside exposure for 12 hours in a temperature of 10° F. Mr. Coxhall relates that, in the famous balloon ascension made by himself and Glashier in 1862, just before they had reached their greatest altitude and while Glashier was lying exhausted in the car; he wished to let out the gas, and on removing the thick glove from his hand to do so, his fingers were frozen the moment they touched the wire.

It is definitely proved that the temperature falls as we ascend above, and rises as we descend below, the surface of the earth, and that the magnetic intensity is least at the equator and greatest at the poles; also that the tensity in the magnetism in different bodies varies according to their form or shape. If the body be oblate or an oblong spheroid, the intensity is greatest at the poles, and still greater if it be of a cylindrical form with conical or pointed ends, as we have before noted. The *depth* of the electric fluid on an angular conductor increases in rapid proportion on approaching the edges, is still further augmented at the corners, which may be regarded as two edges combined, and is a maximum if the conductor have the form of a point, thus exhibiting at each change a greater *condensation* of the fluid.*

When a fine point is used to produce a dis-

---

* Noad : Text Book of Electricity, pp. 18, 19.

ruptive discharge from a positively charged conductor the brush discharge (from the conductor) gives place to a quiet, phosphorescent, continuous glow covering the whole end of the wire and extending into the air. Faraday covered, with a beautiful and luminous glow, a brass ball one and a quarter inches in diameter.* Several instances are reported in which the electric spark has been drawn from a natural magnet. It was done by Faraday and also by Prof. Forbes of Edinburgh in 1832. By the use of a powerful lodestone he succeeded, repeatedly, in producing the sparks.† This experiment is important as further proving, if such proof were necessary, the identity of the action of natural and artificial magnets. The identity or *oneness* of condition of the electric and magnetic forms of power is abundantly manifested. Thus, unlike magnetic lines when *end on*, and when similar poles are face to face, repel each other; *unlike* electric currents when in the same relation, also repel each other; *like* magnetic forces when end on *coalesce;* like electric forces do the same; like electric currents end to end, do not add to their sums, and like magnetic lines of force do not increase each other; lastly like currents side by side add their quantities together, and like magnetic forces do the same,"‡ all of which we have before set forth.

* Noad, p. 36. † Id. p. 303. ‡ Id. p. 271.

Has magnetism any dynamic, mechanical force? Faraday reminds us that when a magnet, either artificial or natural, is in a quiescent state or state of rest the magnetic force exists, is latent in the magnet itself and in the surrounding space just as decidedly and efficiently as when the magnet is excited by any exterior influence. The moment it is so excited its mechanical power is at once manifested. If the like poles of two magnets be approached to each other each repels the other. Metallic contact may be forced but it is not possible to force a contact of the opposing, polar forces. If the positive pole of a natural or artificial magnet be moved at a right angle toward the positive end of a magnetic needle, the needle will be deflected more and more as the approach is nearer. If opposite poles are approached to each other they will draw themselves together and finally clasp and cling to each other with a force that cannot be overcome except by the application of a still greater force. A horse-shoe magnet will draw its keeper to it across a certain distance in space and after contact they cannot be separated except by a force greater than the potential of the magnet. Ganot's disk placed in a certain position in the magnetic field requires a very strong force, comparatively, to move it. In all these cases a mechanical force is as perfectly exhibited as in the application of steam to the piston of a steam engine. The tail of a cat is a perfect illustration of the mechanical action of magnetism. When the animal is quiet its inertia, its state of rest is perfect. The moment the animal becomes excited by fear, fright or friction, the magnetic force, the mechanical action, is immediately and strongly manifested. The relation between magnetism and chemical action, light and sound has been abundantly established by Dr. Thomas Young, Sir Humphrey Davy, Prof. Tyndall, Ganot and others, and Prof. J. W. Draper concluded " that electrification exercises an apparent control over all the phenomena of capillary attraction."

"There are," says Grove, "few if any chemical actions which cannot be made experimentally to produce electricity."

In relation to gravity, the last of the natural forces we proposed to consider and which Faraday so earnestly but vainly strove to co-ordinate with magnetism and electricity, we can only define it under our hypothesis, as a magnetic force operating constantly in one direction, that is, toward the centre of all suns and planets and the centre of the stellar systems to which they belong.

Grove,* can conceive of no other relation between gravitation and other forces, than that it is identical with pressure or motion. Mosotti considered gravitation as identical with cohesive attraction, and cohesive attraction is closely allied to,

* Correlation of Physical Forces, Youman's Edition, pp. 171–2.

if not identical with, chemical attraction or affinity. The identity of cohesive and magnetic attraction is strongly indicated by the fact, shown in so many instances where death has resulted from accidental contact with strongly charged electric wires, that if a person seizes such a wire with the bare hand the hand and the wire will be at once so strongly glued, stuck together, that they can only be separated by detaching, tearing the flesh from the hand. We have already noticed a similar effect produced by clasping with moist fingers, an intensely cold wire charged, according to the new theory, with negative magnetism. Plücker showed that crystalline bodies are definitely affected by magnetism. "There is scarcely any doubt that the force which is concerned in *aggregation* is the same which gives to matter its crystalline form; indeed, a vast number of inorganic bodies, if not all, which appear amorphous are, when closely examined, found to be crystalline in their structure. We thus get a reciprocity of action between the force which unites the molecules of matter and the magnetic force, and through the medium of the latter the correlation of the attraction of aggregation with the other modes of force may be established." Considering gravity as a form or modification of magnetism we may repeat and add to, the reasons that induce the conclusion that it is so. We repeat the following extracts:—I., from Helmholtz: "It has *actually been established* that *all* the forces of nature are measurable by the same mechanical standard and that *all* purely *motive forces*"—of which gravity is one—" are, as regards performance of work, equivalent." This is not identity, but it is equivalence, which is of nearly the same value and is more significant than analogy.

II. From Leibnitz: "The ultimate source of all motion is the original force lying in all bodies which may be restricted or limited in various ways by the conflict or collision of other bodies. This force lies in *all* substances and a certain action always arises from it," and also that "the whole interchange of forces is simply the result of a greater or less movement on the part of the *universal force* which *every atom* possesses, and *all* forces are therefore correlated with *each other* through motion."

The very definition of gravity, the *attraction of gravitation*, indicates its co-relation to magnetism, for there is no other natural force-chemical affinity, cohesion, aggregation and capillary attraction being recognized as correlatives of magnetism—that attracts or repels other bodies. The earth, according to Gauss,* as before noted, is an enormous magnet of immense power. Were not the magnetic force the dominating force of gravitation the planets and their satellites—to revive a very venerable idea—could not be retained in their orbits. " The force by which the earth dominates the moon is the same force by which the sun dominates the

---

* Gauss: Intensity of Magnetic Force.

earth and the moon and also all other planets and satelites connected with our system." * To these extracts from Helmholtz and Leibnitz and Gauss we add the declaration of Sir Isaac Newton, made in his famous 3d letter to Bentley, to wit: "Gravity *must* be *caused* by an *agent* acting *constantly* according to certain laws; but whether this agent be material or immaterial I have left to the consideration of my reader." There is but one force in nature "acting constantly" and freely and that is the magnetic force which is the all-sufficient "agent" to cause the constant action of gravity.

"However if by this or any other argument you have proved the finiteness of the universe, it follows that all matter would fall down from the outsides and convene in the middle. Yet the matter in falling might concrete into many round masses like the bodies of the planets; and these by attracting one another, might acquire an *obliquity* of descent by means of which they might fall, *not upon the great central body, but upon the side of it and fetch a compass about, and then ascend again by the same steps and degrees of motion and velocity with which they descended before,* much after the manner that the planets revolve around the sun, but a *circular motion in concentric orbs about the sun they could never acquire by gravity alone.*"

The Italics are ours, emphasizing the fact that

* Gauss: Intensity of Magnetic Force.

"gravity alone," in Newton's opinion, could not give the planets a "circular motion" "about the sun."

It is evident that the action of gravity considered as mere avoirdupois is zero, except in one direction, and this entirely independent of rotation. We can satisfy ourselves of this fact by the following considerations: Let us suppose the sun and all the planets, in their normal condition, to be inclosed in a metallic cylinder, say ten octillions of miles long and standing perpendicular to the plane of the ecliptic, so that up and down shall be above and below that plane. Then let us suppose the space within the cylinder to be converted into a perfect vacuum, and that, at the same instant, the ends of the cylinder shall be hermetically sealed, and further, that the enclosed bodies shall be at once deprived of their magnetic energy and become simply inert.

From what we know of vacua, it is certain that the enclosed bodies would begin to fall and would continue to descend until they reached the bottom of the cylinder. If the centre of gravity in each body were below the centre of figure, as it necessarily would be, then no rotation or change of direction would be possible.

Let us now imagine that, just before reaching the bottom, the cylinder should be instantly removed and the magnetism and atmospheric air that had been temporarily removed should be instantly restored. Then the released bodies would resume their usual proper motions, rotating on their axes and revolving in their orbits.

The tides are a perfect demonstration of the existence of an attracting, drawing, levitating force. Without the direct action of such a force they could not exist. Gravity as mere weight can produce no such effect. Now, since it is certain that unlike magnetic poles attract each other and that we neither know, nor can excite, in matter, any other force that may be inherent in, or can be imparted to, them that can attract or draw them towards each other, we can only conclude when we see two material bodies so attracted or drawn, that the acting force must be magnetic.

Treating of comets, Sir John Herschel says: "Beyond all doubt the widest and most interesting prospect of future discovery which their study holds out to us, is that distinction between *gravitating* and levitating matter, that possible and indisputable demonstration of the existence of a repulsive force co-extensive with, but enormously more powerful than the attractive force we call gravity, which the phenomena of their tails affords."

"These forces are specially *polar* in their action between particle and particle of indefinitely minute dimensions.* We have no knowledge of any *polar* forces except those that are magnetic.

* Familiar Lectures, p. 140.

"Solar light and solar heat," says Tyndall,* "lie latent in the force-gravity—which pulls an apple to the ground." But light and heat are both forms of magnetic force; hence, if Tyndall is right, the three forces are correlative.† "Created simply as a difference of position of attracting masses the potential energy of gravitation was the original form of *all the energy* in the universe." If this be true, then magnetism is a correlative of all natural forces.

According to Kirschoff the sun consists of a solid or *partially liquid* nucleus in the highest state of incandescence. The number of dark lines measured by Angstrom and Thalen amount to 1000 in which they found a coincidence with the Fraunhofer lines, of more than 460 bright lines of iron. This large preponderance of the most magnetic of substances indicates the strong magnetic power of the sun.

From the foregoing facts and considerations there seems no alternative left but to conclude that the *sun is a magnet*. If we concede the sun to be a magnet and gravity to be a form of magnetic force, we have at command an easy solution of all physical phenomena.

We are hardly at liberty to suppose that the two last statements above were intended to be of a

* Heat as Motion, p. 453.
† Thomson and Tait, in Good Words, quoted by Tyndall: Heat as Motion, p. 453.

mere general character, without specific meaning. The distinguished and most competent physicists who made them were specially treating of forces in a most comprehensive manner, Prof. Tyndall of Heat, and Messrs. Thomson and Tait of Electricity and Magnetism. They certainly would not forget a force so conspicuous and important as gravity.

VIII.

Transcendental Magnetism; World System; God in Creation; Swedenborg; Kant; Nebular Conglomeration; World-stuff; Semi-spiritual Substance; Attributes of God; Spiritual Effluence; Primordial Matter; Rotary Motion; Spirit, Mind and Matter; Extra-stellar space.

LET us now consider magnetism in what may be termed its transcendental relations, in which we may define it as the connecting link between mind and matter, or rather as the medium by and through which the Divine Energy is imparted to all matter, is made effective in the outer-stellar spaces when and as far as the Divine Mind shall direct.

We know that magnetic energy is influenced by distance; that is to say, having a stationary magnet at any given point if we place a magnetic needle near it, two of the opposite poles will be drawn together. Now if we move the magnet away from the needle the magnetic force is diminished as the distance between the two is increased, until, finally, the magnet ceases to attract the needle. The energy of the magnet reaches its limit. If, now, we substitute a more powerful magnet, it will influence the needle at a still greater distance; and so on indefinitely. Hence if we have a magnet of infinite potency it will influence a needle placed at an infinite distance from it. If we have an infinite spiritual energy influencing any other form of matter than a magnetic needle the result will be the same. We may suppose that the primary exhibition of this energy was an exercise of God's will; a divine effluence from infinite power, an emanation from pure spirit.

The origin of this, and some cognate ideas, is very old. According to Anaxagoras, B. C. 500, the primitive condition of things was a heterogeneous commixture of substances which continued motionless and unorganized for an indefinite period. Then Mind began to work upon it, communicating to it motion and order. The Mind first effected a revolving motion at a single point; but ever increasing masses were gradually brought within the sphere of this motion, which is incessantly extending farther and farther the infinite realm of matter." *

A little later Leucippus and Democritus— "maintained that space was eternally filled with atoms actuated by an eternal motion. The weight of the larger atoms forced them downward, while simultaneously the lighter ones were

* Alex. Winchell: World Life, etc., p. 552.

thrust upward. Mutual collisions produced lateral movements. Thus rotary motion was generated which, extending farther and farther, occasioned the formation of worlds." These views, somewhat varied, were extended by Epicurus and the Roman poet Lucretius.

At a much later date—1733–1734—we have the voluminous and complicated speculations of Swedenborg. A very fair summation of them is given in a letter of Mr. T. F. Wright to Prof. Winchell,* as follows: "You will there notice that the idea is that creation is by the self-subsisting God; that His infinite love and wisdom demanded the universe; that its production was not by extension of the infinite nor by the extension of nothing, but by the determination of the infinite into recipient forms produced by itself by degrees, each of which was the medium of creative energy to that next below; that this process terminated in matter; that this gradation was, is and always will be, the vehicle of transmission of life from the Divine; that the preservation exemplifies the creation; that the production of forms of life on earth was through the production of their spiritual prototypes when the time came for it in the process of development; thus, that the evolution was subject at every point to the creative process."

Omitting the views of Mr. Thomas Wright, referred to by Kant, we come to the grand the-

* World Building, etc., p. 571.

sis, the sublime speculations and reflections of Kant himself, to which we have before made slight reference. We make a few quotations from a summary of them given by the late Prof. Alexander Winchell.*

"I assume," he says, "that all the matter in the solar system, in the beginning of all things, existed dissolved into its elements, and filled the entire space of the system. Its existence is an outcome of the Divine Mind. It was endowed with a tendency to form, through natural development, a more perfect constitution." . . . "The cosmical fabric, through its immeasurable magnitude and the endless variety and beauty which shine forth from it on all sides, impresses us with silent amazement. . . ."

The stars are centres of other systems like our own. They are composed of the same elementary particles. Like the planets of our zodiac, they are arranged in a limited zone which we style the Milky Way. "The Milky Way is the zodiac of the higher world orders." But even beyond the bounds of the system of the Milky Way, are other firmamental systems—other Milky Ways. We contemplate with amazement their faint figures pictured on the concave vault of heaven. One might

---

* World Building or Comparative Geology, the most excellent and exhaustive treatise on the subject extant, from the standpoint of the advocates of the nebular and vortex theory.

well conceive an endless succession of mutually disconnected world systems; but such a plan would not provide for the perpetuity of order; and unless the common principle of attraction extended through the entire universe of matter, there would be wanting that character of persistence which is the mark of the choice of God. But a universal co-ordinating principle implies one common centre, and one vast central mass of matter. Here the process of creation began. From this middle point it has extended continually outward over the infinite chaotic waste of unorganized material atoms. I know of nothing that can lift the soul of man to a nobler amazement than the outlook over this boundless field of Almighty power. Worlds rise into being upon worlds in endless progress; and beyond other bounds of the widest realms of order, confusion and chaos forever contend on a field as limitless as if the work of creation had not already attained an endless development. Assign whatever diameter we will to the completed creation we are always near the middle point; beyond the periphery of the sphere, over the infinite expanse, lie buried, in the stillness of the night, the germs of order awaiting the progress of eternity to be quickened into active life. So the process of cosmical organization extends itself. " Creation is not the work of a moment." Millions and mountain-ranges of millions of ages will flow away and " the creation never will be complete.

It was indeed once begun, but it will never end."
.... " Whatever has origin and beginning has in itself the characteristic of its finite nature; it must decay and come to an end. The infinitude of creation is wide enough to spare a world or a Milky Way as easily as a flower or an insect. Meanwhile eternity is adorned by ever-varying manifestations, because God remains active in the unceasing work of creation." But the vastness of objects and events so enstamped with the characters of change and mutability leaves the soul unsatisfied; "it feels a desire to know more intimately that Being whose intelligence, whose greatness, is the fountain of that light which, as if from a central source, illuminates the totality of nature."
" Happy soul if, amid the tumult of the elements and the ruin of nature, it can look down always from its lofty position, and see the current of desolation which brings ruin to all finite things sweep by, as it were, beneath its feet." "When then the fetters which hold us bound to the vanity of created existence, in the moment appointed for the transformation of our being shall have fallen off, then will the undying spirit, freed from dependence on finite things, find the enjoyment of true happiness in communion with the eternal existence." ....
Thus there exists a Being of all beings, an infinite Understanding and a self-existent Wisdom, from which nature, in the whole aggregate of her correlations, derives existence.

Winchell in discussing nebular heat adopts the general impression that it arises from the aggregative process (pp. 93-4) " that the process of conglomeration affords an explanation of the intense heat which vaporizes " the nebular matter. " But," he says, "even yet the mystery of beginnings hangs over us. We have not yet seen molecules rolling themselves up into visibility. We have never, even in imagination, seen atoms emerging from the dread abyss of nothingness. Let us explain all we may ; let us seek out all antecedent conditions possible, enough still remains to pique our curiosity and awe us by its mystery. Nay, the farther we trace the links of the chain of causation, the more palpably we feel the need of some support which is *not* one of the links in the chain, but is superior to the principle of finite causation, and is self-sufficient, existing out of relation to succession, time and space."

"It thus appears that the hypothesis of nebular conglomeration explains two otherwise inexplicable phenomena—nebular amorphism and nebular heat. A third phenomenon hitherto mysterious and unexplained is equally accounted for. That is the *rotary motion* which sometimes arises in nebular masses. This difficulty has often balked belief in the nebular theory of the origin of the solar system." According to Hemholtz,* " the general attractive force of all matter must, however, com-

* Interaction of Natural Forces. Youman's ed. p. 231.

pel these masses to approach each other and condense so that the nebulous sphere became incessantly smaller, by which, according to mechanical laws, a motion of *rotation* originally slow, and the existence of which *must be assumed*, would gradually become quicker and quicker." Thus he *assumes* what Winchell claims is unexplained.

In a "cosmical speculation" Winchell writes: "The universal world-stuff is scattered generally through boundless space. . . . . Out of this semi-spiritual substance germinate then the molecules of matter."

The dominant ideas set forth in the last few pages are:

I. That, scattered through boundless space is a universal world-stuff, a semi-spiritual substance out of which germinate the molecules of matter.

II. That from these are formed nebular conglomerations or masses, accompanied by intense heat.

III. That hence resulted rotary motion, a phenomenon hitherto assumed and unexplained.

IV. That the "mystery of beginnings" still hovers over us.

Let us consider them in reverse order.

Deity in its essence is inscrutable, in its action not wholly so.

We have (*supra*) referred to the attributes of God, His omnipotence, omniscience and a qualified omnipresence. This latter we conceive to be a quiet cognizance, and elementary consciousness ever and instantly responsive to the Divine Will. It is not nothing, it is an emanation from the Godhead, an effluence from the Divine embodiment, the spiritual, personal magnetism of Deity. We have its analogue in the Saviour's life. " And Jesus said, Somebody hath touched me, for I perceive that virtue hath gone out of me.* As many as touched his garment's hem were made perfectly whole." †

It is the infinitesimal something from which primordial matter is evoked or evolved, it is the primary element of creation, it is the germ of every material growth from the atom to the molecule, from the molecule to the mountain, from the mountain to the star. It is the life principle of every living organism since no such organism can exist independent of its agency. There is but one force or form of energy that can fulfil these conditions. It is magnetism.

As bearing upon this point we make an extract from the interesting work ‡ of Dr. James R. Nichols, noticing the death of a patient of the late Dr. Clark of Boston, as described in an essay entitled "Visions," to which Dr. Oliver W. Holmes wrote an introduction. Dr. Clark says that the lady "after saying a few words, turned her head upon her pillow as if to sleep; then unexpectedly turning it back, a glow, brilliant and beautiful exceedingly, came into her features, her eyes opening, sparkled with singular vivacity; at the same moment, with

* St. Luke viii. 46.   † St. Matthew xiv. 36.
‡ Whence, What, Where, Boston, 1883.

a tone of emphatic surprise and delight, she pronounced the name of the earthly being nearest and dearest to her, and then, dropping her head upon her pillow as unexpectedly as she had looked up, her spirit departed to God who gave it. *The conviction forced upon my mind that something departed from her body at that instant of time, rupturing the bonds of flesh, was stronger than language can express.*"

Dr. Holmes referring to this case says, "Dr. Clark mentioned a circumstance to me not alluded to in the essay. At the very instant of dissolution, it seemed to him, as he sat there by the dying lady's bedside, that there *arose something*,—an undefined yet perfectly apprehended somewhat, to which he could give no name, but which was like a departing presence." Dr. Holmes further says, "I should have listened to the story less respectfully, but for the fact that I had heard the same experience almost in the same words from the lips of one whose evidence is to be relied upon; with the last breath of the parent she was watching, she had the consciousness that something *arose*, as if the spirit had made itself cognizable at the moment of quitting its mortal tenement."

Let us now express in our human phraseology the condition and action of the primary forces. Deity is the grand centre and positary of all forces, all forms of energy, a force and energy that are immanent, ominant, positive. Here then is our omnipotent magnet. Its spiritual effluence goes out and is diffused in all directions. As its distance from the grand centre increases, its potency, by a divinely imposed condition, is diminished; it grows less and less until it becomes a negative force. As the distance between the asymptote and curve of the hyperbola constantly diminishes but never becomes zero, so this divine effluence constantly diminishes as it retreats from its central source but never reaches zero, although it ceases to be luminous.

Sir Isaac Newton wrote as follows, Principia, Book III., p. 314. "And now we might add something concerning a certain most subtle spirit which pervades and lies hid in all gross bodies, by the force and action of which spirit the particles of bodies mutually attract each other at near distances and cohere if contiguous; and elective bodies operate to greater distances, as well repelling as attracting the neighboring corpuscles; and light is emitted, reflected, refracted, inflected and heats bodies; and all sensation is excited, and the members of animal bodies move at the command of the will, namely, by the vibrations of this spirit, mutually propagated along the solid filaments of the nerves, from the outward organs of sense to the brain and from the brain to the muscles." His theory of the emission of light, however, has been superseded by the undulatory theory.

We have quoted the views of Swedenborg and Kant concerning the evolution of matter through the agency of the Divine Will, which all philosophers and physicists admit to be the sole and central source of all power. The nidus of the natural forces is magnetism. Its action and functions are regulated by fixed laws. A distinguished poet and essayist * writing without a scientific purpose sets forth some important scientific truths, namely: "Everything in nature is bipolar or has a positive and negative pole. There is a male and a female, a spirit and a fact, a north and a south. Spirit is the positive, event the negative pole. Will is the north, action the south pole."

Let us imagine Deity, Infinite Power, as occupying alone infinite space, a condition that is conceivable. Says Sir Thomas Browne: †—" Before the creation of the world God was really all things." " Before the mountains were brought forth or ever the earth and the world were made, thou art God from everlasting and world without end.‡ If this condition had continued and God had remained inactive there would have been no entity independent of his personality. A limited portion of space could have been occupied only by the radiant undulations of the Light Ineffable. How, then, came matter? By the action of God's will upon the spiritual effluence from the Godhead. Matter is the incarnation of Spirit, as is irrefutably proved by the birth of the Saviour, who was conceived by the Holy Spirit and born of a Virgin."

* R. Waldo Emerson : Essay, Character.
† Religio Medici, p. 374 Bohn's Edition.
‡ Psalm xc. v. 2.

Treating of "Life in Matter" Lotz writes: *
"With this hypothesis of unextended atoms, we
have removed the only difficulty that could prevent
us from giving ourselves up to the thought of an
inner mental life pervading all matter. The indivisible unity of each of these simple beings, that
in it the impressions reaching it from without are
condensed into modes of sensation and enjoyment.
All that stirred our interest in the content of sen-
tience may now have a place of objective existence
in these beings, and numberless events ascertained,
not directly by sensation, but on the circuitous
path of scientific investigation, need not now be
lost, but may, within the substances in which they
occur, be converted into much glow and beauty of
perception to us unknown. All pressure and tension undergone by matter, the rest of stable equilibrium and the rending asunder of former connections, all this not only takes place, but also in taking place gives rise to some enjoyment, each several
being entwined with various reciprocal actions
into the whole of the world, is, in the words of our
greatest national thinkers, a mirror of the universe,
from its place feeling the connection of all things
and representing the special view which it yields
to that particular place and standpoint. No part
of being is longer devoid of life and animation;
only a certain kind of activity, the motions which
adjust the states of the one to those of the other,

* Microcosmos, Vol. I. Book III. Chap. IV., p. 360.

are twined like an external mechanism through the fulness of the animated creation, conveying to all, opportunities and incitements to the various development of the inner life.

"In this sketch," he says, "we indicate a conception of whose spiritual truth we are convinced, yet to which we can hardly expect any further concession than, that among the dreams of our imagination it may be one of those which do not contradict actual facts." *

How completely and admirably the spiritual, transcendental magnetism fulfills these conditions and energizes the vital links of the chain that binds every organism to the Omnipotent Will.

Hence the evolution of the universe. Hence also, by the further exercise of the Divine Will organic laws were established in accordance with which every combination of matter, solid, liquid and gaseous, and every form of life, animal and vegetable, was developed.

Says Hegel: † "The whole normal process of history, to which all the life of man, in Family, in Civil society and State, is organic, consists in the progressive realization of concrete human freedom, that is, of the essential spiritual nature of man through the conscious recognition of God as the

*Microcosmos, Vol. I. Life in Matter, Book III. Chap. IV. p. 360.
† Ethicality, § 270.

foundation of all the true life of the human spirit, and of the Divine Will as the true substance or content of the human will. In the whole process of history or of the 'ethical world,' humanity is progressively learning, and showing that it is learning, that its true language is 'Lo, I am come to do Thy will, O God.'"

He also writes : * "History is the formation of spirit into deed, into the form of immediate actuality. Hence the phases of the development as immediate natural principles."

Star-dust, world-stuff, suns and planets were first developed. In due time, after these last were sufficiently matured, the various forms of life were evolved, the lower forms first and these succeeded by the higher, the last and highest being man, who derived his spirit, his mentality, direct from Deity.

"The spirit of man is the candle of the Lord." Prov. xx. 27.

"The spirit itself beareth witness with our spirit that we are the children of God." Romans, viii. 16.

"There is a spirit in man and the inspiration of the Almighty giveth them understanding." Job, xxxii. 8.

"And I will put my spirit within you and cause you to walk in my statutes." Ezl. xxxvi. 27.

"— for the spirit searcheth all things, yea, the deep things of God." I. Cor. ii. 10.

After referring to birds, fishes, other animals

* Ethicality, § 346.

and man, the Psalmist says (civ. 30). "Thou sendest forth thy Spirit, they" (men and animals) "are created."

The mental power in man is called reason, in brutes, instinct. They are the same in kind, different only in degree. Man exercises his instinct before he does his reason. He first gains knowledge by experience and afterward by observation and instruction. If this were not true he could exercise no influence, could gain no control over other animals. He could establish no friendly relations with them. He could not even teach a dog his name. There could be no trained elephants, no trick horses or mules, no tame lions or tigers, nor any talking birds. There are innumerable authentic records of the reasoning, logical capacity of animals, of their friendly and disinterested actions.

Thus in relation to mind and matter we have given a conceivable explanation of the "mystery of beginning" referred to (*supra*) in paragraph IV. It will also serve to elucidate paragraph I. as to "world stuff" and "semispiritual substance." Paragraphs II. and III. relate to the intense heat produced by the conglomeration of nebular masses and the resulting "rotary motion." In our own stellar system we know that outside of the atmospheres of the sun and the planets the space is totally dark and intensely cold. This must also be true in the interstellar space in all stellar systems.

And this condition must be more emphatically true of the extra-stellar space, since there is there, no matter, nothing to be consumed or to be subjected to frictional force except the spiritual effluence above noted. Necessarily it is impossible that any heat should be evolved. The darkness and the cold are at their maximum. Neither is there any rotary motion except as we will endeavor to explain.

Sir Isaac Newton inferred "from some crude observations" that the power of a magnet decreases in the triplicate ratio of the distance. At a more recent period Coulomb has shown that the law of attraction and repulsion is inversely proportional to the square of the distance. Magnetism, however, as a terrestrial force is very eccentric in its action and is manifested in many ways and under many peculiar conditions by reason of its connection with the densest forms of matter. In the celestial space it is more uniform in its action.

How then did the Divine mind secure the development of "a more perfect constitution" and subject it to the "working of a single general law?" We know that the potency of a given magnet is diminished according to a fixed law. When the potency has reached its limit it becomes negative. If now a stronger force be applied to the border-limit of this exhausted force its action will be renewed and this action will be directly proportional to the force applied.

Let us now suppose that the divine effluence is diffused in all directions to such limit as God chooses to assign and that, when by His Will it is energized into matter, he then imparts to every atom of matter its potency, its affinities and its function. Some of the atoms are positive, some negative, some diamagnetic and some of them, like nitrogen, are neutral. Although all matter is more or less magnetic, still in all forms of matter some molecules are more highly charged, are more potent than others. So also there is a wide difference in the chemic force of different molecules and the facility with which they unite. Some require more or less time to effect a thorough combination, less time for a simple mixture. Consequently when two molecules are attracted to each other the instant they come in contact a gyratory motion ensues the direction of which is determined by the most potent molecule which is almost invariably positive. Thus motion is set up, friction occurs and heat is developed. The two combined atoms in their course meet with a third atom having an affinity for one of them; it at once unites with the pair and joins in the gyratory evolution. Thus agglomeration is effected, motion and heat increase and finally, under the operation of fixed laws and with the lapse of time, worlds are developed. Suns and planets are formed. They are moving in space in obedience to a single form of energy and all of them in one direction, from left to right and with a *rotary motion.* Thus we have shown the origin of that motion which, according to paragraph III. (*supra*) has been "hitherto assumed and unexplained."

We will now state the facts that furnish irrefragable proof of the truth of our conclusion.

All the planets revolve in their orbits from left to right.

The sun rotates on his *axis* in the same direction.

All the planets except Uranus and possibly Neptune rotate on their *axes* in the same direction.

All the satellites revolve in their *orbits* in the same direction, those of the planets Uranus and Neptune excepted.

The moon rotates on its *axis* in the same direction and no satellite is known to have an axial rotation in a contrary direction.

If a magnetic current is made to descend, from the North Pole a magnet placed vertically, it will rotate the pole from left to right.

If a magnetic line of force moves from the North Pole along the path of a polarized ray of light, it will rotate the ray in the same direction.

Water discharging from faucets or other apertures, or escaping from funnels, wash-bowl or bath-tubs, invariably gyrates from left to right, provided the edges and inner surfaces are smooth; and it is immaterial what the shape of the aperture is.

If two different liquids or gases, having mutual

affinities, are presented to each other they unite and rotate from left to right.

The gyration of liquids may be shown by dropping a tablespoonful of dark-colored French brandy into a tumbler of water.

When molecules of oxygen and hydrogen—both permanent gases—come in contact, combination is readily effected, aqueous vapor is formed, and by the high diffusive power of hydrogen is rapidly diffused in every direction, resulting ultimately in rain-drops and fresh-water rivers and seas. The addition of sodium—one of the most abundant of the natural elements—and chlorine develops the salt seas and oceans. Oxygen being strongly magnetic, determines the left-to-right gyration of the compounds.

IX.

Experiments in Magnetism.—Effects of Cold; Sanitary Effects; Effect on Growing Plants; On a Steel Spring; Hunting Dogs; The Sense of Smell; Birds of Prey; Vis-viva of Soaring Birds; Keenness of Vision; Sense of Touch; The Horse.

HAVING a small horse-shoe magnet, and wishing to test the effect of temperature upon it, I attached to the keeper—a small thin piece of bright iron— by a silk thread, a small basket, in which I put as many shot as the magnet could sustain, the basket and shot weighing ten ounces. The thermometer in the room standing at 70° F. in a cold January evening I put the magnet outside on the window-sill, where the mercury stood at 10° F. Taking it in early the next morning it sustained 4 oz. additional weight. I tried this experiment repeatedly, the volts always increasing as the temperature decreased. Possessing a Kidder battery of 5 cells by the use of three and four of them when troubled with catarrh and weakness of voice, both were relieved and strengthened at once by application of the electrodes, covered with moist sponge, to the throat. Weakened vision was also strengthened by application of the same electrodes to the eyes.

Desiring to test the effect of magnetism on growing plants, I selected in a conservatory two pots of colias, the plants of the same age and size, with variegated leaves in high colors. Having thoroughly pulverized a strong lodestone, the plants were removed from the pots, fresh earth put in, and a cavity scooped out in the centre. The roots were placed in this cavity in each pot, one of them properly packed with a mixture of six parts of rich earth with one part of comminuted lodestone, and the other with the rich earth only. They were placed on the bench in their usual position and treated alike. In three months the first was more than one-third larger than the other, and the color in the leaves was brighter. I then selected four pots of the same size, filled them nearly full of rich earth and scooped a cavity in each one. In the first I put 6 grains of wheat, in the second 6 grains of rye, and covered both with a mixture of 1 to 8 of rich mold and pulverized lodestone. In the other two I put wheat and rye in the same way and covered them with rich loam only. The four pots were set together in the open air and treated alike. The grain in the lodestone pots germinated earliest, grew most rapidly, was tallest and of brightest color. As the pots were not large enough to mature the stalks, no grain was produced.

Two years after our experiments, we found the following item in a public journal:

"M. Spechneff, a Russian agriculturist, electrified the seeds of peas, beans and rye, for two minutes, by passing a current through them. The result was that the plants which sprang from the seeds thus treated were much more vigorous than those from unelectrified seeds. He also electrified the soil by burying plates of zinc and copper in it so as to make what is called an "earth battery." The plates were connected above ground by an iron wire. The result was an astonishing crop. A radish grew over seventeen inches in length and five and one-half inches thick; a carrot grew ten and one-half inches in diameter, and weighed six and one-half pounds."

Another of our own experiments was made with a steel spring 21 inches long, $\frac{3}{8}$ of an inch wide and 1-64 of an inch thick. It was marked off into 3-inch spaces. Each division mark was lightly touched with the positive end of a lodestone hammer $2\frac{1}{2}$ inches long and weighing $\frac{1}{4}$ of a pound. The needle of a small pocket compass responded to each division mark. After a touch of each mark with light pressure the needle vibrated more actively, and after a small tap on each mark the needle was rotated entirely around at each division line as the compass was moved from end to end of the spring. After several smart raps in quick succession, the needle was still more vigorously rotated. I treated both arms of a carpenter's iron square in the same manner with the same result.

This experiment in connection with the experiments recorded on page 39 suggested the probable action of hunting dogs in pursuit of game. The earth and all vegetable fibres are conductors. The fox or the hare when not alarmed travel leisurely over the roads, across the fields and through the woods, making an impact on the surface such merely as their weight would give. When alarmed they start upon a run and a smart blow is given at every leap. So, when the hound first starts out for the game he moves cautiously in different directions until he gets the clew, then he advances a little more confidently until he recognizes the stronger track, when with his utmost vigor, he runs reynard or the hare to cover or the ground. The terrier does the same for the rodent and the pointer and setter secure their game by the exercise of the same faculty. We know that both the dog and the cat are very magnetic animals, as we may readily infer from their physical constitution. Oxygen, the most magnetic of all gases, is found in the blood of all animals, and Speilman found in the ash of brain—substance particles of matter that were attracted by the magnet-iron or manganese—and Laër found peroxide of iron, 0.5 to 1.85 in hair, indicating its magnetic character. We also know that the sense of smell in some dogs is very acute. Every one who has had experience with hounds and terriers, pointers and setters has observed this fact. He has seen a hound or terrier in full chase on a certain line, halt instantly, change direction and pursue the new course with the same speed and confidence, even when he doubles on the track of the game. There seems no explanation of this except that their nasal organs are most sensitive magnetic poles, and that, with the wisdom of unerring instinct they " follow their noses." " Reason," says Burke, " often errs ; instinct never."

But there is a perception, an instinct still more acute than this. We know with what rapidity and how extensively odors are diffused through the gases and through the atmosphere, many gases being themselves highly odoriferous and penetrating. Here we have, apparently, a key to another of nature's secrets ; that which enables birds of prey to find their game and animals to seek each other's society. The eagle, the hawk and the raven follow, with unerring certainty, the track of death and decay. It is an impressive sight to watch the eagle, as we have repeatedly done, when he leaves his eyrie to seek food for himself and his royal mate, who is attending to her domestic duties while incubating the eggs that are to furnish the heirs to the lofty throne. Leaving his perch he sweeps from it as a centre in a wide horizontal curve, perhaps ten miles in diameter, which serves as the base of a spiral in which he continues his flight constantly ascending, each curve being more contracted than its predecessor until he suddenly leaves it and strikes a tangent downward for a distant point. One of two reasons has determined his course. He has two senses of great penetrating power in his eyes and nostrils. In his upward flight both are intensely active, the first in searching for fields where lambs, hares, fowls or other small game may be seen; the other to detect odors that are in the air. If he sees the game he starts directly for it; if he detects an odor he follows it to the carrion from whence it emanates.

The soaring flight of the condor, the eagle and other birds of prey furnishes peculiar and interesting evidence of an inherent energy that produces motion without apparent action. The eagle while performing his spiral ascent vibrates his wings only in the first few curves of the spiral, after which by some magnetic *vis-viva* he literally *soars* upward with outstretched wings. When he first turns on his tangential flight he vibrates his wings for a moment, then bringing them to a poise, he rushes down with a constantly accelerating velocity. The condor's long-sustained soaring and floating capacity is well known. No more delightful, exhilarating and less fatiguing mode of motion can be imagined. It is not surprising that the popular fancy should suppose wings to be the motors of the angelic host.

The hawk is apparently more indebted to his eyes than to his nostrils for his supply of food. I saw an interesting instance of this while standing on the bridge over the rapids of the American channel in the Niagara River just above the Falls. A fish hawk soaring some 1200 feet above, suddenly descended into them, seized a mullet some six or eight inches long and rose again into the air. After reaching an altitude of eight or nine hundred feet he lost his hold on the fish, which, of course, began a fall of constantly increasing velocity. The hawk instantly turned in pursuit and recaptured the fish before it struck the water. As his wings were folded this violation of the laws of gravity must have been due to the fact that the bird, the *living* matter, exerted some inherent power, some natural *vim* that enabled it to accelerate its downward motion while, at the same time the distended air bladder of the fish may have slightly retarded his motion. St. John de Creve Cœur in his "Travels" in upper Pennsylvania in 1798, describes a similar scene and gives a pictorial representation of it. A hawk, having risen in the air with a fine pike, is set upon by an eagle and compelled to drop his game, whereupon the eagle starts for and secures it before it reaches the water. In these cases the birds may have been aided by a magnetic *vis viva* different from mere gravity.

The horse gains knowledge both by touch and

smell. If he fears, or has an aversion to any particular object, as a buffalo-robe or open umbrella, let it be carefully, gently presented, to him so that he can touch it with his lips and smell it at the same time, and his fears will be quieted, never after to be excited thereby. His lips are his fingers. If he fears a pokerish stone or stump, let a man sit upon, or stand near it, and make any motion that will indicate his presence, and the horse can at once be led up to it, as we have proved experimentally.

The inter-cranial organ of smell is more largely developed in the lower animals than in man. In birds, however, it is very small and hence its acuteness with them is the more remarkable. It is also remarkable in some aboriginal races. Humboldt informs us that the Peruvian Indians know by smell when a stranger is approaching, and before he is sufficiently near to note his complexion, whether he is a European, or an Indian or a Negro. Late experiments in hypnotism prove that the sense of smell is greatly intensified in those who are subjected to its influence. The experiments of Charcot and Bernheim in France and of Braid in England have shown some astonishing developments.

In one case a visiting-card was torn into strips and given to a lady who was hypnotized, her eyes being closed as in sleep. After she had smelt repeatedly of one of the strips, they were all hidden in different places in another room, more than forty feet distant. She then found them all, smelt of each piece, placed them together in proper order and read correctly the name on the card.

X.

Force ; Energy.

IN treating of the influence to which matter is subjected in order to produce changes in its position, condition or action, we use the term *force*, not because, in all cases, it is most appropriate, but because it is appropriate in the greatest number of cases, and for the further reason that it is already habilitated in the vocabulary of scientific terminology. Mayer's definition of "force" is "something which is expended in producing motion." English physicists propose to condense this into the single word "energy" and to allow the word "force" to retain the meaning which it bears in common language. Energy, however, is, scientifically, more exact.

In our citations we have set forth quite fully the strong conviction entertained by the most eminent physicists that there must be a unification, so to speak, of forces, and that there must be one predominating force of which all the others are modifications or variations, and we quoted the arguments and facts designed to establish this postulate.

Of course the grand, primeval origin and source of all power, of all force, is the everlasting, almighty, omniscient God. Says Meyer—" Force of Inorganic Nature "—" The first cause of all things is Deity—a Being ever inscrutable by the intellect of man." All other powers and forces of every kind, form and degree are derived from this one supreme force, and are differentiated from it by certain fixed, unchangeable laws—unchangeable except by the will of the Lawmaker. Among these are the forces of nature, so called, which we are permitted to investigate, analyze and utilize.

In treating of magnetism, we specialized and emphasized its power, its condition and its action, and particularly its correlation with other forces, We showed its universality, its presence and influence over all forms of matter, its constant, inherent energy, attractive and repulsive, accretive, disruptive and explosive; the amazing and indissoluble connection between its poles, the impossibility of producing one of them without at the same moment producing the other, and the marvellous range of activity between these two extremes from the faintest spark of the Leyden jar to the thunderbolt that rends the mountain and shakes the earth; from the slight chill that condenses the dew-drop to the intense temperature that solidifies the mountain torrent and builds up the resistless glacier that plows its rocky furrow down the mountain side.

The conclusion at which we arrive is that all the other forces of nature are, more or less, dependent upon this force, whether considered as a monad or a dyad, and that all the other natural forces, electricity, light, heat, gravity, sound, chemical affinity, capillary attraction, repulsion, attraction, disruption amd explosion are modifications of it, or are influenced by it.

Some physicists prefer to assign this predominance to electricity. It matters little what we name the first term of the series provided we get correct results. Faraday proved the actions of magnetism and electricity to be alike and calls them " analogous." Grove proved the same fact and calls them " correlative but not identical." " But," says Helmholtz,* " there are still other natural forces which are not reckoned among the purely moving forces—heat, electricity, magnetism, light, chemical forces, all of which stand in manifold relation to mechanical processes. There is hardly a natural process to be found which is not accompanied by mechanical actions or from which mechanical work may not be derived."

The agency of heat in nature is almost universal, and it either primarily occasions or materially influences all the different changes that take place upon our globe.

* Popular Sci. Lec. translated by E. Atkinson, p. 162.

"It is capable of *altering* most of the *colors* of bodies, and it is perpetually producing numerous decompositions and new combinations upon every part of the surface of the globe.* We have before shown (p. 70) the action of magnetism on vegetable colors. There are results that can be produced by magnetism that cannot be produced by electricity. But there are two other cardinal facts which effectually differentiate the two forces. The first is, that electricity, except in its modified form of heat or light, cannot traverse a vacuum. It may be forced through, but cannot freely traverse it. This magnetism does in any vacuum however perfect."

The second grand fact is that we can get no electric action unless we *manufacture* it so to speak. [This will be deemed utterly erroneous by those who claim that " electricity is never created or destroyed " but " is simply moved and strained like matter." Is it then matter or analogous to it?] Two or more substances are indispensable and must be used to secure electric action. If it is desired to obtain currents of frictional electricity the amber, the sealing wax, the glass rod, the silk and woollen fabric must be procured, and then the necessary physical force must be applied to develop the currents. Another method of producing the electric current is through the proper arrangement and physical manipulation of the Voltaic pile.

* Sir H. Davy, Works, Vol. II., pp. 393-97.

If the static or Faradaic current is sought, the metallic cylinder, the iron core, and the silk-covered copper wire to form the coil must be prepared and properly arranged, then the *manufactured* battery must be connected before the current can be generated. With a little less labor, but still labor, a current can be obtained by induction or by impact. In all these cases it has been necessary to *manufacture* the electric action, or obtain it by artificial appliances.

But the magnetic force, magnetism, is self-existent, constant, always ready. From the sun, the lodestone, the atmosphere, the earth, it leaps instantly into life under proper conditions, manifests its presence and performs its work, on the land, in the sea and in the sky. The sphere of its activity is everywhere, in everything, in all conditions of life and in all forms of matter. It pilots the mariner safe through the stormiest seas in the darkest nights; utterly blind itself, it safely leads all who see; it clicks the seconds on the clock of time and with invincible power and unfailing constancy it swings the pendulum of eternity and wheels the planets in their orbits and the stars in their courses. With its mighty arms extended from a common centre, with its positive right hand and its negative left, it rotates around each other, orbs that are billions of miles apart. And yet, for centuries men have debated whether it "acts at a distance" or can be considered as a physical force. Faraday, having the courage of his convictions, pronounced it a force and demonstrated the existence of "physical lines" of "magnetic force." His great contemporary, Mr. Clerk Maxwell, who demonstrated mathematically the correctness of Faraday's propositions, advanced a step farther and hints at its existence, in a certain sense, as *matter*. These are his words: "In fact a theory of *magnetic matter*, if used in a purely mathematical sense, cannot fail to explain the phenomena (of magnetism) under certain conditions." * If it is not matter it is inherent in all matter. If it is not force, or energy, it is absolutely essential to the efficiency of all force or energy.

"In heat of varying temperatures different degrees of magnetic force are manifested. It is always magnetism either active or latent." Faraday showed that "iron and nickel, when heated to a degree far above that required to render them insensible to an ordinary magnet, still pointed axially between the poles." And we may again call to mind Faraday's declaration that oxygen is a *magnetic substance*, its magnetic force being in proportion to its density. Hence if it were absolutely solid it would be the most perfect of lodestones. "In warm-blooded animals it is more or less active; in cold-blooded animals more or less latent."

If our conception—mark the *if*—of the nature of magnetism be accepted as correct, we may study

* Elec. and Mag. Vol, II. p. 6.

the correlation of other forces with it. Light is reflected magnetism. Projected from the sun it passes through the total darkness of the ether and the partially rarefied gases lying between the atmosphere of the sun and the earth and is only made manifest when it strikes the earth, whence it is reflected back, makes our atmosphere, and the hemisphere of the earth exposed to the sun is always luminous—solar light. Electricity is *condensed* magnetism. It is identical with light during its passage through the ether. The resistance of friction condenses it and converts it into caloric. The more obstinate and complete the resistance the more intense is the caloric produced, as is abundantly demonstrated by the electric arc light. The intensest power of magneto-caloricism is exhibited in disruptive discharges.

We have stated in our preface that, after finishing our notes on the properties of magnetism, we had seen, for the first time, Hodge's Modern Electricity, in which he says, p. 123 : "The commonest way in which electricity makes its way through a gas, setting aside the mere mechanical conveyance by solid matter, is that of disruptive discharge." This is especially true of nitrogen.

Further, he says: " The atoms of a particular substance—iron, for instance, or zinc—have an electric whirl "—magnetic, we should call it—" of a certain strength circulating in them as one of their specific *physical* properties." (P. 149.) We can predicate nothing concerning physicality, if we may use the term, nor of materiality independent of matter. All matter can be infinitely expanded and rarefied, or compressed and condensed. We know that magnetism, light, sound and electricity, since Hertz's experiments, can be compressed, condensed, and reflected or refracted.

XI.

Disruptive Force.

The most terrific results of the magneto-calorific force are manifested in disruptive discharges. The "freaks of lightning," as they are very appropriately called, are of frequent and familiar occurrence, and often of a most singular character. At times, several persons standing near each other are all instantly killed. Again, a mother, sitting with a child in her arms, is instantly killed, while the child remains uninjured. A large mass of material in a building or other form is, in a few moments, reduced to ashes. Again, another mass of matter is instantly shivered into fragments, without a sign of ignition on any of them.

Harris reports the case of an English ship, whose main-mast, weighing 18 tons, was three feet in diameter, 110 feet long, and strongly bound with iron hoops, some of which were half an inch thick and five inches wide, yet it was shivered to pieces by an electric bolt, and the hoops burst asunder and scattered around amidst the fragments of the mast.

We were once within a few rods of a beautiful pine tree, 50 feet high, with a bole 16 inches in diameter, a wide-spreading, ovate top, standing near a rustic walk. A thunderbolt, that shook the buildings in the vicinity, reduced it instantly to fragments, not one of which was equivalent to a piece a foot long and an inch in diameter, and not one of them was even scorched.

The bolt sometimes produces clairvoyant effects. There is an authentic account of an intelligent farmer, who, in a cloudless day, was leading his saddled horse across a pasture. A thunderbolt burst suddenly over his head, instantly killing his horse, gave him a shock that threw him to the ground, but did him no injury. His eyes were closed, but his mind was perfectly clear. Through the back of his head he saw the horse fall, and could see objects all around while the shock lasted.

The fact that nitrogen, in some form, is the chief ingredient in artificial explosives seems to confirm the belief that it is largely present in thunderbolts.

Confirmatory of this view is the fact stated (*seq.*, p. 129), that, the higher we ascend from the earth, the more nitrogen and the less oxygen we find.

Earthquakes, tidal-waves, cloud-bursts, cyclones and hurricanes, all are results of the disturbance, greater or less, of the earth's magnetic equilibrium, external and internal. When sun-spots are largest and most active, and when the sun and moon are then in conjunction with the earth, this disturbance is at its maximum and its effects are most destructive. And there is every reason to believe that this disturbance is increased by the vast number of iron and steel rail-tracks, telegraph, telephone, electric and trolley wires running in all directions over the land and under the water in all parts of the world. Very strong, almost conclusive evidence of this fact, is found in the greater frequency of magnetic storms, cyclones and hurricanes, and the less frequent displays of the Aurora Borealis. These two last phenomena—cyclones and hurricanes—are exhibited more frequently by day than by night. It would be interesting and useful if the Weather Bureau would systematically note their recurrence, as also the auroral displays.

XII.

Light—What is it?

LIGHT is the most wonderful, beautiful and useful of all the phenomena of the universe. The announcement of its origin is the most sententious, sublime utterance in any language. *God* said, let there be *light*, and there *was* light. There could be neither tree nor shrub, neither bud nor blossom nor fruit, without light; the earth would become a desert without light; there can be no color revealed to us without light; the seven-fold glory of the prism could not be developed without light; the richest odors are born of light. The fragrance of hot-house flowers is far inferior to that of those which lift their fragrant palms to the cloudless blue. Light paints the lily, perfumes the violet, and gives its blush to the rose; it flashes in the diamond and nestles in the ever-changing tints of the opal; it reveals the bloom on beauty's cheek, and beams in the love-light of her eyes; it glows in the early dawn, and robes in a blaze of glory the sunset hour; it portrays, actinically, each feature of the warm summer landscape, and glorifies the foliage of the autumn woods; it fills, like a benediction, all the air of a sweet Sabbath in June; it fairly revels and dances in the gorgeous plumage of birds and the brilliant scintillations of insects' wings; it sparkles in the morning dew-drop, and, with all the rich, prismatic hues, it portrays upon the rain-drop screen the sign of God's eternal covenant of peace with man. We know it in more phases and it blesses us in more ways than any of the other phenomena of nature. And yet, what is it?

If an individual could be miraculously endowed with a body that he could move in any direction by his own will, and a mental power that could continue active and efficient under all conditions and that could endure all possible alternations of temperature, if such a person at noon, on a cloudless day were to start directly toward the sun, shining in all its meridian splendor, what would be his experience? After leaving the earth he would feel the pleasant excitement of a bird on the wing until he reached an elevation at which the air, becoming more rarefied by the loss of one proportion of its oxygen, would become converted into exhilarating gas, since the higher we ascend the more nitrogen and the less oxygen we find. Breathing this in the mild radiance and soothing serenity of the charming temperature, he might believe that he had reached the Elysian fields.

But as he pursued his upward journey, the air, according to the present theory, would become still more rarefied, and if he were in his normal condition, the blood would ooze from every pore in his flesh and dissolution, with swift descent earthward, would follow. But, preserved by his miraculous endowment, he would continue his ascent and soon reach a region where the air is still more rarefied and the light would begin to fade out of it, turning first to a ghastly white, then to a steel blue, then to a violet, then to indigo and finally to the blackness of darkness. Then too, being marvellously sustained, he would find himself intensely cold, in an atmosphere in which Icarus might have safely used his waxen wings. Nevertheless he would be cheered by a faint gleam of light, because the dark rays which are streaming towards the earth from the sun would be intercepted by his body and he would be surrounded by a halo, a slight luminous atmosphere. " However intense a beam of light may be," says Tyndall (743, Heat as Motion), " it remains invisible unless it has something to shine upon to *reflect* it." Again (753), "the blue light of the sky is *reflected* light, and were there nothing in our atmosphere competent to *reflect* the solar rays, we should see no blue firmament, but should look into the darkness of infinite space." Our aerial traveller will soon find himself within the resplendent atmosphere of the sun. What force carries the light rays through the "darkness of infinite space?" Let us emphasize this supreme, cardinal fact; that there is but *one* independent self-acting force that can accomplish this result. That force is the *magnetic force*.

If the light of all suns were extinguished the planets would still continue, for a time, to rotate on their axes and revolve in their orbits. The magnetic energy is as potent in total darkness as in the most brilliant sunlight. It guides the ship as safely at midnight as at noon-day.

XIII.

The Experiments of M. Hertz.

"The great interest," says M. Joubert, "of M. Hertz's experiments lies in the accurate information that we gain from them concerning the intervention of the external medium in electrical phenomena. The idea of this intervention is not new. After Faraday's experiments and Maxwell's theories, there remained no doubt on this point in the minds of physicists; but the experimental proof was wanting. This has now been given by M. Hertz. His experiments show particularly that the medium which intervenes in electrical phenomena is the same ether that forms the seat of luminous phenomena; that the disturbances in both kinds are set up under the same conditions and with the same rapidity; and lastly that there is identity between certain electrical phenomena and the luminous phenomena," a grand fact that almost fully answers the long and earnestly pondered question "what is the ether?"

"The effect of an electrical current may be represented as follows: Suppose a conducting wire to be connected with any number of elastic cords of indefinite length, radiating from all parts of its surface. By the passage of a current through the wire its force will be exhibited diamagnetically and will be imparted to all the cords at their points of connection, and they will be drawn forward in the direction of the main current and will be placed obliquely to it and will so continue as long as the current is maintained. When the current is withdrawn the cords assume their normal position. As the cords are of indefinite lengths the electrical effect is extended to any distance. . . . As we know that time is a function in the transmission of currents, the current in this case is transmitted to the different cords successively." M. Hertz estimates that it would require eight minutes to reach the sun, about the velocity of light.

Continuing and varying his experiments M. Hertz found that the magnetic electric waves traversed walls of stone and passed through the closed door of a partition; that the propagation of the current was the same as that of light and that the current was subject to the same laws as those of light, another grand fact that will aid us still further in solving the great mystery as to the nature of the ether. As the currents are sent through these cords to distances *proportioned to the power applied, it must follow that with infinite power they would traverse infinite distances.*

This action of the currents may be accurately represented by the tail of a cat, a highly magnetic animal as we have before noted. When the animal is in a quiet condition the filaments or fibres of fur make a slight angle with the axis of the tail, but when the animal becomes greatly excited, these fibres immediately assume a position nearly at right angles with the axis; and when the excitement ceases they assume their normal position. Here again, is a natural magnetic force absolutely identical in its character and in its action with the magneto-electrical force.

Another of the most singular or rather *unique* discoveries of Hertz, was an electro-dynamic shadow, cast by an iron post, showing that electricity, like light, may be refracted. This discovery may remove ghosts from the category of myths, and place them in that of visible but intangible realities. Perhaps the next step in this direction will be the construction of a magneto-electro-dynamic lens with which, properly arranged in a Kodac case, we may secure counterfeit presentments of the wandering spirits of the night.

The most significant lesson we learn from M. Hertz's experiments, is the very intimate relation between, if not identity of, the ether, the magneto-electric and the luminous forces.

Concerning the peculiar vibratory discharges of the Leyden Jar, which were long such a mystery to physicists, and which have been so well shown in the recent beautiful experiments of Prof. Hertz, it is notable that the late Prof. Joseph Henry recognized and demonstrated their action. They touch directly the long mooted question of " action at a distance," and also the still longer mooted question " what is the ether?" Says Henry,* " In extending the researches relative to this part of the investigations, a remarkable result was obtained in regard to the distance at which inductive effects are produced by a very small quantity of electricity; a single spark from the prime conductor of a machine of about an inch long, thrown on to the end of a circuit of wire in an upper room, produced an induction sufficiently powerful to magnetize needles in a parallel circuit of iron placed in the cellar beneath, at a perpendicular distance of thirty feet with two floors and ceilings each fourteen inches thick intervening." The author, Henry, is disposed to adopt the hypothesis of an "electrical-*plenum*." (Ether, magnetism?) Emphatically a *plenum*, all stellar space being permeated with it and all matter amenable to it. In the sequel we give some further illustrations of the prevalence and value of magnetic forces.

* Scientific writings of Joseph Henry, Smithsonian Institution, 1886.

XIV.

Animal Magnetism.

WE are well aware that scientists, particularly Electricians, do not recognize animal magnetism as a legitimate branch of science. Nevertheless, there is no branch of science the truths of which have been more thoroughly demonstrated by long and patient investigations and by almost innumerable and varied experiments. In the sequel we have quoted many cases and authorities that establish its verity. Our own experience, related in the sequel, is a perfect demonstration of its existence and action. We are familiar with the action of magnets and magneto-electricity, and therefore speak confidently and understandingly on this subject.

This form of magnetic force—animal magnetism—differs somewhat from that exhibited by cataleptics, and the victims of delirium tremens. For some years past this force has been most remarkably manifested by Mrs. Abbott, the Georgia wonder, so called, a young woman of petite, delicate physique, but sanitarily sound, intelligent and modest in demeanor. Of course, she can give no explanation of the amazing force manifested through her slight frame.

We give a few incidents of her exhibitions which have been witnessed by thousands of interested spectators in all parts of the world. At the commencement of an exhibition six or eight of the most healthy athletic men in the audience are invited on to the stage to act as judges and subjects. Any one or all of these may attempt to resist the mysterious force under various conditions. A single person may hold out at arm's length a cane or umbrella, and brace himself as strongly as possible to maintain his position. By simply putting her hands on the cane or umbrella, and apparently without making the least physical effort she pushes him all about the stage and he cannot by any exertion stand still if he wishes to. Per contra, Mrs. Abbott will hold out, in the same manner, a cane, or in order to make room for more persons to grasp it, a billiard cue. Then, standing on one foot only she invites them to move her. Four stout men, two on each side of the cue, make the most determined effort to push or pull her from her position. The struggle is vain. Apparently they could as easily move an iron lamp-post. Three strong men hold a chair between them, and Mrs. Abbott asks them to press it to the floor. They cannot do it. The judges balance themselves on the hind legs of a chair without touching it with their hands. Mrs. Abbott with a hand on each side of the sitter's head lifts him and the chair from the floor. Each sitter declares that he feels no hand pressure on his head, and it will be borne in mind that he has no hold of the chair.

These performances were successfully varied. We have related them for the purpose of suggesting an explanation. We have heretofore quoted Faraday's statement that, "if a copper disk, suspended by a long string, is set whirling, and is then introduced into the field of an electro-magnet, its motion will be instantly arrested and it cannot be further rotated in the field." Further rotation is impossible except by the destruction of the apparatus. We have also quoted Helmholtz's statement, that a copper disk, set in motion in a wood frame with multiplying gear and rotated with great rapidity, was placed between two pieces of iron which did not touch it, being part of the armor of an electro-magnet. Turn the current of a three-cell battery around the magnet, and the pieces of iron act like a break that entirely stops the rotation of the disk, and it can only be started again by the application of a strong force.

In both these cases the resistless force that controls the disks is a magnetic force, pure and simple, since there is no contact, no impact, no friction. These disks are said to have weighed from one quarter to half a pound. They were amenable to the magnetism of the earth and the atmosphere only. We know the great potency of the terrestrial magnetism and that the high magnetic condition of oxygen makes atmospheric air a magnetic medium of no small power. The emphatic point connected with these disks is their *fixity* under the conditions in which they are placed. And in this fixity they furnish a striking analogy to the phenomena exhibited by Mrs. Abbott.

As a mass of matter she weighs, instead of a quarter or half a pound, about 110 pounds. The hair of her head, and every hirsute appendage of her body; all the nerves, muscles and tendons of her body, her blood highly charged with oxygen, all these are magnetic conductors, more or less effective.

In the case of the disks, when the magneto-calorific current is discontinued, their fixity is at once removed and their freedom of motion restored.

What is the motor force that enables the living machine to manifest its power? The dynamo that does this must be her will. She stands on one foot with the billiard cue held, with both hands, directly to the front; it is seized by four powerful men who strive desperately, but in vain, to move her from her position. She ceases to exercise her will, and then either of the men could toss her out of the window.

One man holds a chair horizontally to the front, and two others add their strength to his in an effort to force the chair to the floor. They do not succeed while she wills that they shall not. She ceases to do so and the chair can be dropped at once.

A heavy man tilts himself back upon the hind legs of a chair with his hands folded on his breast. She gently places her hands on the sides of his head, and without exerting any recognizable pressure, she lifts him, with the chair, nearly breast-high from the floor. If she were to remove her hands and fully relax her will, *if she were to shut off the magneto-calorific current*, both man and chair would at once fall to the floor.

There is no opportunity here for legerdemain or connivance. The subjects do not know what is expected from them until they go upon the stage. The conditions for the exercise of the brute force —the strength of the men—are of the most favorable character. There is no contact with the corners or sides of the room. The abnormal power of the woman is exhibited in visible, open space. In one case she stands on one foot, like a light column standing on one end. And yet the brute force applied to the opposite end cannot move it.

XV.

The Brain, Its Structure, Functions and Action.

IN addition to the effects of animal magnetism heretofore described, we propose now to consider the operation of that force as connected with the most perfect organism known to us, and especially with that most marvellous piece of mechanism which dominates it—man and the human brain. Since the experiments of Gall and Spurzheim, and more particularly of David Ferrier, the structure of the brain has been very satisfactorily delineated and its functions described. A general indication of its parts and their functions is all that is necessary for our purpose.

Concerning a certain "conception" as to the "place of the soul," Lotze writes,* "According to it, the soul would, at a single point at which its activity had reached its maximum, extend its influence directly over all, but with diminished force over different parts of the body. Supposing this diminution to take place rapidly indeed, yet with

---

* Microcosmos, Vol. I. pp. 297, 298, 299.

so moderate an acceleration that its effects were still perceptible at a sensible distance from the maximum point, there is no actual phenomenon that favors such a supposition. The afferent operation of the sensory, the efferent activity of the motor, nerves always cease however near to the central organs their connection with these is severed, and no trace is ever to be found of any direct action of the soul extending outwards even so far as to pass over the trifling interval created by a fine cut between two immediately adjacent elements of a nerve. . .

"Any one, however, cherishing the hope that more minute observation would find some such limited seat of the soul could not but acknowledge that it has been sought for in a wrong way. Slendder as is a single nerve-fibre, a point of common intersection for all could not be an indivisible point, must be a cubic space with a diameter of quite appreciable magnitude. This space must be under the soul's direct control; within it we would not expect to find isolated nerve-filaments continued; their isolation could only serve to bring the physical processes taking place in them, without any intermingling, into the soul's sphere of action. When they have arrived there, their farther separation is unnecessary; for in the soul itself there are no partition-walls dividing the different impressions, and it must be capable of holding their multitudinous variety, without confusion, in the unity of its being. This cubic space, the seat of the soul (by our supposition, *seq.*, the pineal gland), would then have to be conceived either as filled up with a parenchyma without fibres and somehow homogeneous, throughout which nerve-stimulations are propagated in all directions, or as a cavity along whose sides, and within the distance to which the soul's immediate efficiency extends. All the nerve fibres—or a sufficient select number of them—require to pass though not to terminate. . . It—the soul—is in direct reciprocal action only with the brain ; there accordingly, it has its seat, in the sense which the word ought to have."

In response to this we give the following exposition of the brain which indicates the pineal gland or conarium as the seat of the soul and supplies the conditions necessary to its activity.

The brain fills the whole cavity of the skull. It is divided into four principal parts, the cerebrum, the cerebellum, the pons-varolii and the medulla-oblongata.

The cerebrum, the upper part of the encephalon, occupies the largest part of the cranial cavity ; its two halves are called the cerebral hemispheres, and are connected by the great transverse commissure known as the corpus-callosum. The cerebrum covers the cerebellum and the olfactory lobes. Its exterior surface is deeply convoluted, and is traversed by many deep furrows or fissures. In some of these furrows the arteries are securely imbedded. Nature here furnishes us an instructive lesson : she puts her pipes underground. The interior of the brain is also supplied with an elaborate system of connected cavities called ventricles or cœliæ.

The cerebellum lies below the posterior portion of the cerebrum, by which it is entirely overlapped, and it occupies the lower part of the cranial cavity. By certain peduncles it is intimately connected with the cerebrum. It is globose in form, and its exterior surface, like that of the cerebrum, is convoluted and furrowed, though less deeply and more systematically.

The brain is covered by three membranes, the outer—dura, the middle—arachnoid, and the inner —pia. The substance of the brain is of two kinds, gray, gangliose or cellular nerve-tissue, and white, commissural or fibrous nerve-tissue. The gray matter forming the outer layer of the cerebrum and the cerebellum is also called the cortical substance to distinguish it from the white or medullary substance that constitutes the deeper portions. The brain may be designated as a collection of ganglia united by white commissures. Besides the cortex there are several ganglia or collections of gray matter in the interior, as the corpora-striata, the optic thalami, the optic lobes or corpora-quadrigemina, the corpora-dentata of the cerebellum and the corpora-olivaria of the medulla-oblongata.

The cortex of the cerebral hemispheres is the

portion of the brain in which the most complex mental co-ordinations are effected, and which is most directly involved in mental acts. Certain parts of the cortex are called sensory or motor centres. But in fact, the cortical or gray substance is the principal and beginning of every motion in both the cerebrum and cerebellum.

The corpus striatum is shown to be connected with the nervous force passing downward, and the optic thalamus with that passing upward; among the latter that of sight is connected with the posterior part of the thalamus. The anterior optic lobes are also involved in the sight function and the posterior in the auditory.

The cerebellum is connected with the muscular and voluntary actions, while the medulla-oblongata contains numerous centres whose functions relate to vaso-motor action, cardiac action, respiration, deglutition, etc.

According to Winslow,* the medulla-oblongata embraces all that part of the brain which occupies the middle portion of the base of the cerebrum from front to rear—anterior and posterior—and also the middle portion of the cerebrum. It forms a medullary base between the cerebrum and the cerebellum, common to both and generated by the reciprocal continuity of these medullary substances and separated from both by the transverse process

* The Brain, by Swedenborg, quoted by Tafel, p. 302.

of the dura-mater. The medulla-oblongata may therefore, he says, be justly considered as the third general part of the whole mass of the brain, or as the common production of the whole medullary substance of the cerebrum and the cerebellum. Heister (p. 304) considered it as giving origin to the spinal marrow and the nerves of the brain. The pons-varolii occupies a central portion of the base of the brain near the substance of the spinal cord, and connects together the three larger parts of the brain. Says Quain, " It forms a prominence marked by transverse fibres above and in front of the medulla-oblongata and between the lateral hemispheres of the cerebellum."

In the lower part of the brain, in the sella-turcica, lies the hypophysis or pituitary body, a small oval, vascular gland having two lobes, its function being connected with the lymphatic system in purifying and regenerating the blood in its change from the veins to the arteries.

We have reserved to the last a notice of the pineal gland, the smallest member of the cranial system, but whose importance we believe to be inversely proportional to its size. Its location is given as follows : * " Between the globose bodies of the cerebrum and cerebellum and the medulla-oblongata which extends beneath, there is a kind of a triangular, medullary space thrust in be-

* The Brain by Swedenborg, ed. by Tafel, p. 16.

tween, which embraces the corpora-quadrigemina, the pineal gland, the passages underneath and some striated medulla. This space by the ancients was called "isthmus." It is, in a certain sense, the uniting medium between those three bodies: above it thrones the cerebrum with its two hemispheres, below it rests the cerebellum, and around it, at the sides as well as behind, extends the medulla-oblongata.

It will be remembered that these are the three major and most important members of the brain, whence, it will be observed, that the gland occupies the crowning position in the encephalon, the centre of its nervous parts with all which it is intimately connected, especially with that most important pair of masses the optic thalami. And its location in respect of the cerebrum, the royal member of the cranial system, is precisely similar to that of the oculus fundus of the eye, the most sensitive and delicate point in the retina.

In size, the gland is larger than an average pea, and is slightly conical in form, whence it is sometimes called the conarium. It consists of a number of follicles lined by epithelium and connected together by ingrowths of connective tissue.

Lancisi, quoted by Tafel, says that its least glandular follicles secrete a lymph and a liquid peculiar to the nerves, such that they seem to constitute a peculiar cortex of a diminutive brain, and that, for this and other reasons, we may, without any injustice, call the pineal gland the cerebellum of the cerebrum itself.

While the functions of all other parts of the brain have been satisfactorily determined, such is not the case as to the conarium. In late researches by H. de Graff and Mr. Baldwin Spencer they endeavor to show that, in certain animals, it represents part of a rudimentary visual apparatus.

The gland is so diminutive in size, so difficult to reach, so impossible, successfully to vivisect, if we may use the term, that little has been learned of its functional character. The only other method of learning something about it, is by post-mortems. But even this field is wonderfully barren. We have been unable to add to the two cases reported by Tafel. One was that of a man in middle life, a simpleton who stammered. The cerebrum was found to be white and compact like curd, the collosum a little hard and the gland shrunken to the size of a hemp seed. The other case was that of a virgin twenty years old, who, after six months of great suffering from pains in the head became blind, was gradually deprived of all her senses and died in great agony. The gland had grown to the size of a hen's egg and was petrified.

Now, from what we know of rudimentary bodies in other animals, they possess no such facility of extreme contraction or expansion, nor are they permeated with follicles charged with an abundance of nerve matter and nerves. Nature has already reduced rudimentary members to their least dimensions and their minimum activity. Their nerves are as rudimentary as their physical substance and cannot be subject to acute pain such as was suffered by the young woman whose gland was enlarged and ossified.

From its peculiar position, its abundant supply of nerve matter and nerves, and its firm attachment to the sensory centres of feeling and emotion, we may be permitted to conclude that the pineal gland is more effective in developing feeling and emotion than any other portion of the brain, that indeed, its special function is to develop and express the sublimest emotion of which the soul is capable, that of adoration, worship. Its intimate attachment to the optic thalami is peculiarly indicative of this emotion, the first prompting of it being to raise the eyes heavenward as in the act of devotion.

> " Prayer is the burden of a sigh,
> The falling of a tear,
> *The upward glancing of an eye*
> When none but God is near."

This gland may furnish another illustration of the correctness of Sir Isaac Newton's statement that small magnets are more powerful in proportion to their mass than larger ones. The conarium is the smallest of the cranial bodies; it may be capable of producing the sublimest emotions. It was a reasonable conjecture of Galen and Descartes that the conarium was the seat of the soul.

In the domestic animals which have the conarium fully developed and are still entire strangers to the feeling of reverence, that feeling may be superseded by a sentiment of terror. When such animals are greatly frightened, prompted by fear, they seek safety in flight, but when they are stricken with terror they are incapable of voluntary motion and may be easily slaughtered. They are so overcome with a feeling of awe that they are entirely helpless. We have almost daily experience of the difficulty of removing horses or any other domestic animals from burning buildings.

In wild animals, beasts of prey which are savage and fearless, the feeling of awe or terror may be superseded by feelings of hatred or vindictiveness. Their controlling desire seems to be to attack and destroy every living creature they encounter. In no case do we find reasonable evidence that the conarium is a rudimentary organ.

The chief substance of the brain is the white and gray matter, constituting nerves, nerve-cells, fibres, corpuscles, vesicles, ganglia, etc. The nerve fibres are principally of the class termed white or tubular nerve fibres. The number of them forming the white substance of the brain is counted by hundreds of millions. The nerve cells, vesicles or ganglionic corpuscles are little bodies of a variety of forms. The corpuscles occurring in the nervous substance must also, like the nerve fibres, be numbered by the million. The gray matter of which these corpuscles is composed is considered as the seat of nervous energy, which is conveyed to all parts of the system.*

All portions of the brain are united by innumerable nerves, fibres, fascicules, processes and commissures which anastomose through and inosculate with each other in the most thorough manner.

"There is," says Ferrier,† "practically no limit to the number of associated combinations of sensory and motor elements. Sensory centres form organic association with other sensory centres; motor centres with motor centres; sensory centres, simple and in complex association, with simple or complex association of motor centres. In this variety and complexity of permanent modification and organic cohesions between the sensory and motor centres of the hemispheres, we have the basis of all intellect and volitional acquisitions. Each motor centre may enter into organic associations with each and every sensory centre, each definite association being the representation of some consciously determined act."

The sensori-motor functions of the brain have been quite accurately determined. Those parts upon which the five senses depend, sight, hearing,

* Bain, Senses and Intellect, pp. 13, 14.
† Functions of the Brain, pp. 437, 438.

taste, touch and smell, are well known. We have ventured to suggest the distinct and supreme function of the conarium, the latest scientific term for the pineal gland.

Permeating certain spaces between different constituents of the brain and indispensable to its action is a fluid that Quain calls "a very limpid serous fluid which occupies the subarachnoid space," and Magendie states that this "subarachnoid fluid exists not only in the cerebral canal but also within the cranium, in which it fills up all the space between the brain and the dura-mater.* Furthermore as we learn from Bain,† "both the nerve fibres and the nerve cells are largely supplied with blood, without which they would be lifeless and incapable of action. An important function of the corpuscles of the nerve cells is that they form the grand junction or crossings where the fibres communicate with each other and establish a vast system of lateral and forward connection necessary to the co-ordinating and concentrating movements and sensations in the bodily mechanism associated with mind. ‡

"The machine-like nature of much of the structure and movement of the human body," says Ladd, § "does not escape the most ordinary ob-

* Tafel : The Brain, p. 350.
† Senses and Intellect, p. 16.
‡ Brain, Senses and Intellect, p. 17.
§ Elements of Physiological Psychology, pp. 214, 215.

servation. When this body as a whole or in respect of some of its parts, changes its position in space, its various masses support and act upon each other in essentially the same manner as the masses which compose the parts of any machine constructed by human skill. Such movement is possible for it because its frame-work of bones has a rigidity sufficient to sustain the less rigid organs; and because the bones are so divided and yet articulated that they can assume different relations toward one another in accordance with the simplest principles of mechanics. The laws of the lever, of the pulley, the ball and socket joint, etc., need no modification when applied to this particular machine of the human body. The action of certain other of its parts which do not belong to the bony framework, but which are of muscular or epithelial structure, is also plainly of the same machine-like character. The movement of the heart, for example, is in part to be explained as that of a pump with chambers and valves, and the flow of the blood through the arteries is that of a fluid pumped through conduits of unlike and changeable sizes. So, too, the lungs may be, with considerable propriety, compared to bellows which alternately suck in and expel the surrounding atmosphere." The optical and auditory nerves are mechanical in their action, and the distribution of fluids through the tissues of the body is also a mechanical process. Another mechanical apparatus is exhibited in the system of secretory organs by which the joints and articulations of the bones, tendons and muscles are constantly and effectually lubricated.

We have thus described in a very general way, the arrangement of nerves, muscles, tendons, fibres, tissues and ganglia, and the frame-work of articulated bones which constitute the human body, the human machine. But they would all be ineffective, useless, as before noted, without the presence of the blood. And the most efficient elements of the blood are iron and oxygen, the two most magnetic substances known. Thus the blood may, not inappropriately, be called fluid magnetism. By virtue of that fluidity it permeates and physically vitalizes every part of the human structure. The functional activity of the brain, the nerves, and in fact of every portion of the system is dependent upon it.

What is the psychic force, the motor power that operates this wonderful machine? By our hypothesis it is the will of God operating through certain agencies in pursuance of certain laws. There is an inherent, inherited divinity, a spiritual force in our nature. It is fundamental, underlying, comprehensive, stimulating and directly aiding the development of the will and all our consciousness, all our feelings, emotions and sentiments. Primarily it is entirely independent of experience, but experience is a cardinal factor in its growth and activity.

We have seen that all parts of the brain are connected with each other by innumerable nerves, fibres, fascicles, ganglia and tissues, and that all the members of the body are connected with the brain in a similar manner, and with each other by the addition of muscles, tendons and sinews. The most important of the brain nerves are those connected with the cortical system which are distributed from the brain through the cerebellum and the cerebrospinal axis to the extremities and all other parts of the body.

" The structure of the nervous substances, " says Bain, * " and the experiments made upon the nerves and nerve centres, establish beyond doubt certain peculiarities as belonging to the force that is exercised by the brain. This force is of a *current* nature; that is to say, a power generated at one part of the structure is conveyed along an intervening substance and discharged at some other part. The different forms of electricity and magnetism have made us familiar with this kind of action. . . . This portable or current character of the nerve force is what enables movements distant from one another in the body to be associated together under a common stimulus."

The evidence is overwhelming that all the nerves, muscles, tendons, sinews and tissues of the body are

* The Senses and the Intellect, p. 48.

good magnetic conductors. The currents which traverse them are differently designated as afferent—in-carrying; efferent—out-carrying; inhibitory—intermitting or checking; accelerating—constant or increasing. These conductors are excited and stimulated in like manner with any others, and in like manner, and under the same conditions, they respond. Says Ferrier,* among the foremost of craniologists, " Galvanic stimulus gives shocks; the faradic stimulus continuous stimulation. If the chief object be to secure efficient stimulation, to call forth in a decided and distinct manner the functional activity of the part to which the electrodes are applied, it would matter little whether we used the galvanic or faradic stimulus, provided they were both equally suitable for the purpose. But this is not the case. Not only a certain intensity but a certain direction of the stimulus is necessary to produce the characteristic effect."

Concerning the summation of stimuli in the nerve tract " the law" says James,† " is this, that a stimulus which would be inadequate by itself to excite a nerve centre to effective discharge may, by acting with one or more other stimuli (equally ineffective by themselves alone) bring the discharge about. . . . Single stimuli entirely inefficacious when alone may become efficacious by sufficiently rapid reiteration." This is precisely

* Functions of the Brain, p. 225.
† Psychology, Vol. I., p. 82.

what occurs in artificial currents. Single conductors placed side by side accumulate strength, and a given current is increased in power by rapid impact. Ferrier also notes the fact that the gray matter of the cortex, like nerve centres in general, is capable of *storing up* and responding to a succession of stimuli individually insufficient to excite action.

"With respect to neutral molecular disturbances," writes Ladd, "all nerves are excitable, conductors of excitation and exciters of nerve cells and muscle fibres." According to our hypothesis the most potent " exciter " in all cases is the magnetic force. We have abundant evidence that all nerves, muscles, tendons, sinews, fibres and fluids in all living organisms are amenable to and directly acted upon by this force.

Instead, then, of attributing the vis-viva of the brain and the body to the influence of " nerve exciters," " muscle stimuli," " afferent " or " efferent," " inhibitory " or " accelerating " currents, how much more accordant with the facts would it be to recognize by its proper name the force that produces the result,—the magnetic force, and hence magnetic currents.

XVI.

The Heart, Its Functions and Action.

THE arrangement of the brain, bones, flesh and blood exhibited in the healthy man present a most perfect and admirable model of a magneto-calorific machine. And it is interesting to trace out its physical modus operandi.

We begin with the heart as its dynamo. By its protected nerve-wires it is connected with the brain and with every part of the body. The nerves of the cortical system are the largest and longest, extending mainly up and down from the brain through the trunk and to the extremities of the limbs. From their responses to the magnetic force we conclude that they are paramagnetic, and that the innumerable commissures and fibres that traverse the brain and the ganglia which compose its substance are diamagnetic and diffuse the force in all directions. The heart furnishes the kind and degree of stimulus necessary to operate the machine. " But the rate of the heart beats " says Ferrier,* " is subject to variation through certain nerves connecting it

* Functions of the Brain, p. 98.

with the medulla oblongata; one set of nerves inhibiting or restraining, the other accelerating or increasing the heart's action." Thus these inhibitory nerves of the heart which " run in the trunks of the vagi or pneumogastric nerves " serve as a rheostat to produce rhythmical respiration. . . . . "The accelerator nerves reach the heart through the last cervical and first dorsal ganglia of the sympathetic." Both these sets of nerves can be excited by various stimuli. By the joint action of the two sets the heart becomes a veritable rheotem with its systematic and rhythmatic diastole and sistole.

In artificial conductors we know that the magnetic force can be intensified so as to produce warmth, heat, flame, fusion and gaseous dissipation, the effect being proportioned to the intensity of the friction. In like manner when the magnetic force is coursing through the various nerves of the system, if it is checked, if a lesion occurs, the troubled nerve at once signifies it to the brain. A slight interruption may produce some uneasiness; one more decided, more or less depression, mental anxiety; one still still more emphasized, a severe lesion, produces pain; as this increases it is communicated to other adjoining nerves until finally great distress and agony are experienced.

On the other hand, when the whole system is in perfect order, all the members, nerves and muscles working healthfully and harmoniously, the blood flowing free and pure, the mind agreeably and sedulously occupied, then the exaltation of spirit is at its maximum; a genial flow and glow of feeling quickens the pulse, stimulates the senses and gladdens the heart.

Magnetic action is induced in several ways; by friction, induction and impact or rapping. Man being a magnetic animal every step he takes, every motion of his body or limbs, every movement of his joints excites the magnetic stimulus. We have quoted Ferrier's statement that the gray matter and nerve cells are capable of *storing up* this stimulus. This is done when mind and body are at rest, and especially in sleep. In healthful sleep the mind, body, nerves and muscles are comparatively at rest; the circulation of the blood is slower, as are also the pulsations of the heart which become more regular, rhythmic. Every throb acts as an impact or rap that increases the magnetic force and stores it up in the body. When the physical frame is sufficiently rested and fully recharged with magnetism the subject awakes. Then the first motory prompting is to yawn and stretch his limbs. Thereby the pulsations of the heart and the circulation of the blood are both quickened and he rises refreshed and invigorated in body and mind and with renewed elasticity of spirit. And no person can deprive himself of this needful rest and recuperation of mind and body without consequent suffering and abridgment of the period of life. The heart-dynamo will be steadfast and faithful in the performance of its duty so long as its powers are not overtasked. And in this connection it may be interesting to consider the task that the living heart accomplishes in a stated time.

In mechanics the work done by a machine is usually estimated—by Grove's method—in foot-pounds, that is the number of pounds the machine can raise through one foot, or the number of feet that the machine can raise one pound, *i. e.*, the work equals the weight multiplied by the height. The work accomplished by the heart in twenty-four hours can be estimated approximately in the same way. It amounts to 138 foot-tons, that is, the heart performs in twenty-four hours an amount of mechanical work equivalent to that of a machine that will raise, during the same time, 138 tons through one foot, or one ton through 138 feet.*

In closing it may be well to correct some erroneous impressions concerning the function of this cardinal organ. In every civilized language the heart is characterized in many phrases with many adjectives. They are incorporated, embalmed as it were, in the literature of every nation. There are " feeling," " generous," " bold," " brave," " kind," " warm," " cold," " faint," " true," " false," " bleeding," " broken," " confiding," " doubting," and " ravished," hearts, besides an innumerable multi-

* Chapman. Human Physiology, p. 281.

tude of loved and loving hearts. Indeed love and loving hearts are the invariable constants in the varying phrases and phases of every tongue. They are all very fine, very expressive, very poetic, very romantic. Romance would perish and love would go into perpetual mourning if they were expurgated from the literature of the world.

Nevertheless, they are intrinsically only poetic and romantic. The heart is not a seat of consciousness. It has no sense, no feeling, except of a neural character. Its sensitiveness is intense by reason of its near and strong connection with the brain. It is easily and strongly affected and agitated. It is literally and emphatically a *stout* heart, since we learn from Ferrier* that "the heart muscles contract rhythmically on stimulation apart from all nerves and ganglia. It will beat rhythmically after complete severance of all its cerebro-spinal connections, or even after being removed from the body." Hence it may happen that the faithful heart may continue to beat after the brain is dead.

* Functions of the Brain, p. 98.

XVII.

Gases.

HITHERTO in considering the nature and properties of magnetism and electricity, we have confined ourselves mainly to their relation to and their action with liquids and solids. It is now proposed to consider them in their connection with a very different form of matter—the gases.

As early as 1823, Faraday liquified various gaseous bodies by pressure alone, and later, in 1845,* he condensed still others that were more refractory, by cold and pressure. According to Boyle's law, the pressure exercised by a given mass of gas varies inversely as the volume of the space within which it is confined, or, the space occupied by a given quantity of gas varies inversely as the pressure. All gases, except one, are unsaturated vapors since they *can all be condensed* by simultaneous application of *sufficient cold and sufficient pressure*, confirming Faraday's conclusion that "every gas could probably be liquified by the combined influence of cooling and pressure, could we extend

* Phil. Trans., p. 155.

them sufficiently far." "No man," says Boyle,* "perhaps yet knows how near to an infinite compression the air may be capable of if the *compressing force be competently increased.*"

Independent of the sudden changes produced by the action of chemical affinity, gaseous and liquid forms of matter may be transformed into one another by a series of continuous and unbroken changes.† Careful experiments in condensing gases were made by Cailletet and Pictét in 1878. The latter, after liquifying oxygen at a pressure which became constant at 475 atmospheres, on opening the stop-cock at the end of the tube containing it, saw a lustrous jet of liquid oxygen issue with great violence, whilst around it was a haze of particles of *solid* oxygen. In a subsequent experiment, the presence of *solid* particles in the jet of liquid oxygen was confirmed by illuminating it with polarized light. After subjecting hydrogen gas to a pressure of 650 atmospheres, on opening the stop-cock a steel-blue colored, opaque jet of liquid hydrogen rushed out with a hissing noise, and at the same time a rattling was heard, as if small shot or hail had fallen on the ground.

If the gaseous form of a substance be compressed or cooled so far that any further condensation or cooling will cause the disposition of some of it in the liquid form, it is said to be a vapor.

* Tait, Prop. of Matter, p. 162.
† Andrews's Scientific Papers, p. 317.

The term vapor is often applied in a wider sense to the gaseous form of a liquid or solid substance—as, for instance, ether-vapor, chloroform-vapor and others.*

If hydrogen can be condensed into a liquid or solid it would seem that it can be expanded into ether or some infinitesimal element.

Bancalari first discovered the fact that, on the interposition of a gas or candle flame between the poles of an electro-magnet, the flame was instantly repulsed when the electric current was closed, to return to its first position the instant it was broken. The same result would have followed if natural magnets had been substituted in the place of electro-magnets. Zantedeschi, in verifying Bancalari's experiments, found that this repulsion of the flame happened with contacts of both solid and hollow soft iron, and he was convinced that it was an immediate action of the magnetism on the flame; "a fact," declares Faraday, "of the greatest importance to science," as it truly is; for it proves, in this case, that the action of the natural magnet and of the electro-magnet is precisely the same, and this further proves, if such proof were necessary, that they are identical in character.†

Another most important and abundant of the gases, the lightest of them except hydrogen, is ammonia. Its specific gravity is ·76, that of hydrogen

---

* Daniel, Principles of Physics, p. 216.
† Exp. Res., pp. 491, 492.

being ·70. It may be extracted in great abundance from gas-liquor, and largely, also, from all urinary and organic secretions and excretions, as well as from decayed animal and vegetable matter. When pure, it will not only not support combustion, but its hydro-carbonate, carbonate and sulphate readily yield incombustible gases which possess the positive quality of extinguishing combustion; of course, it is opaque to heat. If inhaled pure, it is fatal to animal life. One volume of water will absorb or dissolve 500 volumes of it. Hence its abundance, under certain conditions, in aqueous vapor.

Hydrogen also occupies an important place in nearly all organic substances. It constitutes, by volume, two of the three parts of water. Water, as vapor, occupies 1,700 times more space than when in the liquid state at ordinary temperatures. Aqueous vapor is continually ascending into the air, and, by reason of its solvent properties, particles of many other substances are carried into the air and distributed over the earth. The spectroscope reveals hydrogen largely in the corona and chromosphere of the sun, and Father Secchi holds that it constitutes the principal element of a numerous class of stars, and is also found in meteorites.

Nitrogen is another important constituent of animal and vegetable life, and it also occurs, though not abundantly, in the mineral kingdom. It possesses no active properties; is, like ammonia, incombustible, and does not support combustion, and, consequently, will not, when pure, support respiration. It does not enter into direct combination with any element except oxygen, and, by the electric spark, with titanium, tungsten, and one or two other substances. It is a remarkable fact that two gases, neither of which will support life continuously, yet, when mechanically mixed in certain proportions, compose the healthful air we breathe, and without which we could not live; and, in a certain other slightly varied proportion, form "laughing-gas," the breathing of which affords the most delightful sensations. As to its magnetism, Faraday characterizes it (§ 2860) as being a very indifferent body, neither paramagnetic nor diamagnetic, but zero or neutral.

Among the important results concerning the diffusion of gases, as reported by Tait,* is the fact that, the higher we ascend from the earth, the more nitrogen and the less oxygen we find.

Another most essential element both as a gas and in its denser form of charcoal or graphite, is carbon, which occurs in great abundance and in a great variety of forms and combinations. It is the only element always present in animal and vegetable substances. Cook—Chemical Philosophy—describes it as " one of the most widely diffused and one of the most important elements in the scheme

* Recent Advances in Physical Science.

of terrestial nature. United to the three aeriform elements, oxygen, hydrogen and nitrogen, it forms the chief solid substance of all organic structures. Combined with oxygen it forms the carbonic dioxide of the atmosphere which is the food of the whole vegetable world." In the crust of the earth it is found in large measures of coal and petroleum, and is an essential constituent of the limestones and dolomites. The spectroscope also reveals it as one of the most important constituents of comets. It is a good conductor of electricity in all its forms except as crystallized in the diamond, which is a poor conductor.

But by far the most interesting, most indispensable of all gases in its properties and its predominant efficacy in all the processes of nature is oxygen. " The magnetic constitution of oxygen," says Faraday (§ 2966) "seems to me wonderful. *It is in the air what iron is in the earth.* Its power in specific magnetism is plus 1.181. Hence oxygen in the air exercises a remarkable amount of magnetic force, especially since its magnetic condition is greatly altered by variations in its density and in its temperature" (§ 2796).

It is stated by Prof. Dewar* that he placed a quantity of liquid oxygen in the state of rapid ebullition in air (and therefore in a temperature of 181° C.) between the poles of the historic Faraday magnet in a cup-shaped pan of rock salt (which is

* "Notes," Nature, Dec. 17, 1891.

not moistened by liquid oxygen and therefore keeps it in a spheroidal state), and to his surprise Prof. Dewar saw the liquid oxygen, as soon as "the magnet was stimulated, suddenly leap up to the poles and remain there permanently attracted until it evaporated."

Though a gas it is apparently like the solid metals, iron, nickel and cobalt, when they are in the range of temperature which affects their magnetic forces, and it may, like them, perhaps, rise by cooling to a very high state. It is a singular fact that iron can only be *permanently* magnetized with the aid or in the presence of oxygen, as in steel. It is a little more than one-tenth heavier than air, and ice-cold water will hold in solution more than four per cent. of its volume while water at 68° F. will only hold less than three per cent., a fact that proves that lowering its temperature increases its density. "It is to an enormous degree the most abundant, as it is in many respects the most important, of the elements of matter upon the earth. The only other element that can compare with it in abundance is silicon, the special element of mineral silicates. It constitutes nearly, if not quite half the total weight of known matter, and silicon not far from one-third. Of water, the liquid part of the earth, oxygen forms a still larger proportion or eight-ninths. Of living matter, vegetable and animal, oxygen also forms by far the largest element.*

* H. Wortz, Johnson's Cyclopedia, Art. Oxygen.

As the question of color may have some interest as connected with the final development of our scheme we may note some of its more important characteristics as revealed in the spectrum of the solar rays and also in the spectra of some of the gases. From Mosotti we learn that the greatest illuminating power is found in the yellow, the central color of what were formerly called the three primary colors, blue, yellow, and red, and that the intensity declines systematically on either side. Its penetrating power is also greatest making it serviceable for signals. Incandescent metals, and rarefied gases enclosed in glass tubes (Geisler's) when made luminous by the electric spark, revealed hydrogen as purple red, chlorine, magnesium and thallium different shades of green, and sodium yellow, and nitrogen blue or purple. Some recent experiments have shown the color of liquid oxygen to be a beautiful blue. The substance that produces a peculiar green line in the aurora, the zodiacal light and the corona of the sun is, as yet, unknown. It may here be noted that Langley and Very[*] found the spectrum of the Italian firefly—Pyrophorus Noctilucus—to be of maximum brilliancy in the *green*. The luminous power of gases increases in proportion to the pressure to which they are subjected, by which their density is increased,[†] as we have before noted.

[*] Silliman's Journal, Vol. 40, 3d Series, p. 102.
[†] Schellen, Spec. Anal., p. 15.

XVIII.

Stellar Systems and Celestial Geography.

HAVING thus studied the forces of nature and ascertained their various forms and properties we have now to consider their application and use in the construction of stellar systems and a celestial geography.

From the earliest dawn of human intelligence the stars have furnished the most absorbing and fascinating field of study and speculation. Both in tradition and recorded history their influence has been recognized, and they have been supposed to be potent in their courses in deciding the destinies of individuals and nations, whether striving against the enemies of Israel among the hills of Judea or guiding the shepherds to the birthplace of the Saviour.

Supposed to be infinite in number and unchangeably fixed in their positions in the celestial vault, it has also been supposed that they were arranged in some orderly system and subjected to some dynamic laws. Hence many hypotheses concerning the structure of the universe have been suggested. All hypotheses fill space with some form of matter, of atoms or molecules. These are supposed to be constantly in motion; some in all directions like snowflakes in a whirlwind, some in fixed directions like drops of rain in a gentle shower; that they possess certain affinities, that they attract or repel each other, and that they are forced into different forms and conditions, gaseous, gelatinous, aqueous, viscous or solid.

The stellar system which has been most favorably received is that of Laplace, Kant and Herschel, founded on the nebular theory, that all suns and planets are agglomerations of nebulous matter, the nebulæ themselves being aggregations of molecules or atoms in the most attenuated possible forms of matter, which are subject to certain attractive and repulsive, cohesive and disruptive forces, which decide their shapes and control their motions.

Some years after the publication of Kant's system an original and more elaborate one was set forth by Johannes H. Lambert, a lucid synopsis of which—not being able to find his original work—I copy from Prof. Newcomb's Popular Astronomy.

"He supposes the universe to be arranged in systems of different orders. The smallest systems which we know are those made up of a planet with its satellites circulating around it as a centre.

The next system in the order of magnitude is a solar system, in which a number of smaller systems are each carried around the sun. Each individual star which we see is a sun, and has its retinue of planets revolving around it, so that there are as many solar systems as stars. These systems are not, however, scattered at random, but are divided up into greater systems which appear in our telescopes as clusters of stars. An immense number of these clusters make up our galaxy and form the visible universe as seen in our telescopes. There may be yet greater systems each made up of galaxies, and so on indefinitely, only their distance is so immense as to elude our observation." " Each of the smaller systems visible to us has its central body, the mass of which is much greater than that of those which revolve round it." This feature Lambert supposed to extend to other systems. " As the planets are larger than their satellites and the sun larger than its planets, so he supposed each stellar cluster to have a great central body around which each solar system revolved. As these central bodies are invisible to us, he supposed them to be opaque and dark. All the systems from the smallest to the greatest were supposed to be bound together by the one universal law of gravitation."

This system is adversely criticised, quite decidedly by Prof. Newcomb, and more mildly by Father Secchi, criticisms which we hope to show are erroneous, and that, on the contrary, the hypothesis contains the germ of a far more sublime stellar cosmography.

As science, in the department of magnetism and electricity, is more indebted to Faraday than to any other physicist, so it is in the department of astronomy more indebted to the investigations and labors of Sir William Herschel than to those of any other astronomer. The Columbus of the skies, with his telescope-ship he traversed with persistent zeal and keen intelligence the celestial seas of space, and discovered for mankind its first new world, together with the numerous nebulous island-groups scattered in all directions around it. He taught us how other worlds may be built up, how we may watch their birth and growth and proximately determine their age, from the youthful star that has not yet reached the period of scintillation to the adult sun that, with resplendent glory, "sweeps in triumph through the signs of heaven."

He insisted on the existence of matter diffused through space, out of which the nebulæ were probably formed; and he noticed the fact, which all astronomers have done, that the southern hemisphere is less richly provided with stars than the northern; and we are led to the conclusion that not only in appearance but in fact the stars are more dense near the galaxy. Among the multitude of nebulæ revealed by his telescope he believed that every stage of the process (of growth) might be considered as displayed to our eyes, and in every modification of form to which the general principle might be conceived to apply. The more or less advanced stage of a nebulæ towards its segregation into discrete stars, and these stars themselves towards a dense state of aggregation round a central nucleus, would thus be in some sort an *indication of age.**

These changes were especially notable in the Magellanic clouds or nubeculæ—note *nu*beculæ, not *ne*bulæ—the former being immense fields of stardust in which the latter appear in a more condensed form. These remarkable regions of cloudlight lie in the southeastern portion of the firmament, and present almost every stage of stellar development from the motes of star-dust floating in space to the largest and most resplendent sun.†

The spectroscope has very materially enlarged our knowledge of the nebulæ by showing that the spectra of some of them have characteristics belonging to the spectra of gases; others have the equally characteristic spectra peculiar to *glowing solids;* while in a third class may be placed all those whose spectra combine the characteristics of both the preceding classes, ‡

* Sir J. Herschel, Outlines of Astronomy, p. 504.
† Sir J. Herschel, Outlines of Astronomy.
‡ H. Abbe, Art. "Nebulæ," Johnson's Cyc.

XIX.

Zodiacal Light.—Comets, Dust of Time.—Spectrum of Gas Flame.

"It is generally agreed," says Mr. Alexander Winchell,* " that this phenomenon † arises from a ring of meteoroidal bodies encircling the sun, nearly in the plane of the ecliptic and probably rotating like the rings of Saturn. But considering that the phenomenon has been so frequently witnessed in the east and west at the same time, it is necessary to assume that while most of the matter lies within the earth's orbit, some portion extends beyond that limit. Accordingly the earth moves within this assemblage of particles. Consequently, unless they have the same velocity as the earth, they must by their collisions offer a resistance to the earth's motion."

COMETS.

"Whence comes the 'Dust of Time'? There is nothing around which the dust of time does not

* In his admirable and exhaustive work, "World-Life or Comparative Geology."
† The Zodiacal Light.

gather. It accumulates among the shelters of mountain cliffs. It falls upon ivy-mantled towers and ruined walls, and creates a rooting-place for many a hardy herb and a nidus for countless living germs. It clogs the water-passages from our roofs, and fills our cisterns with soils yielded by the atmosphere. It gathers about deserted structures; it buries the foundations of columns and temples, and new temples are built upon foundations beneath them. . . . . Whence the dust which has buried walls and towers and cities? . . . . Much of the soil which gathers upon roofs and in the crevices of old walls has been lifted by the winds from bare field and dusty street. Even the snowy summits of the Alps become stained by terrestrial particles borne by upward currents into the mountain air. And yet I will venture the opinion that some dust comes to the earth daily *which had never belonged to the earth before.* Out from the depths of space—beyond the clouds—beyond the atmosphere—from a granary of material germs which stock the empire of the blue sky, comes a perpetual but invisible rain of material atoms—like the evening dew, emerging from the transparency of space into a state of growing divisibility." . . . . Among the first to produce evidence in support of the theory of the cosmic origin of certain portions of the atmospheric dust was Baron A. E. Nordenskjold. He reported large patches of arctic ice covered with a gray diatomaceous powder mingled with grains of magnetic iron surrounded by iron-dioxide, and containing also probably carbon. Similar deposits were reported from snows from the neighborhood of Stockholm, from the interior of Finland and from Spitzbergen. " M. Tissandier," continues Prof. Winchell, "has made quite extensive researches on atmospheric dust, and has put beyond question the meteoric origin of certain portions of it. Many grains and minute globules of iron are met with in these dust-falls, which appear to have been fused. . . . . These grains of magnetic iron have been collected from a great variety of situations—from the summit of Mont Blanc, from rains recently fallen, from the towers of Notre Dame Cathedral in Paris and many other cathedrals, from the borders of Lake Lehman, from the hospice of St. Bernard and from many localities in distant countries." Prof. Winchell gives a number of highly magnified figures of these iron globules and afterward says, " Thus the evidence of the perpetual arrival of foreign matter from the interplanetary spaces seems conclusive."

Dr. Huggins demonstrated the existence of carbon in the comets of Brorson and Winneke in 1868. We hope in the sequel to get better acquainted with their tails.

The orbits of most of the comets are elliptic, and when subjected to the sun's attraction they are drawn towards it with a velocity which constantly increases as the radius-vector diminishes, a velocity at perehelion distance which, for Donati's comet Sir J. Herschel estimates at 200,000 miles a minute.

Notwithstanding this tremendous velocity with which comets are projected towards the sun they are repulsed and turned aside in a different direction. The terrific force which resists these fierce attacks is the magneto-electric force. Says Father Secchi, "It" (gravity) "is not the sole force which rules the universe; perhaps it is itself only a consequence of disturbed equilibrium in the ether. But the comets have given indications of some other force, not yet well defined, operating in space. The rapid development of the tails of these bodies is not explained by heat alone, nor by that of gravity. Magnetism, electricity have been evoked, but as yet nothing as to this is certain."

Langley also suggests that "it is doubtful whether gravity is sufficient to account for the velocity of all comets," and that "it seems certain that it can, in no way, explain some of the phenomena of the tails."

Prof. Lockyer in his recent "History of a Star" says of the tails of comets, "It looks as if these tails may consist, to a large extent, of the gases which exist in meteorites, and which can be driven out of them at not very high temperatures. Seeing that these are thrown off with great velocity, and shine through millions of miles in the depths of space, it is not likely that we are dealing with any such considerable substances as the vapor of iron, magnesium or any other metal. This consideration may help us in the chemistry of the repelling body " (ether).

Sir J. Herschel states that "the matter of the secondary tail in Donati's comet was evidently darted off from the nucleus with incomparably greater velocity than that which went to form the primary one."

Our explanation of this is, that the enormous resistance encountered by the comet as it approached the sun was constantly increasing, and when the material, "consisting," according to Schelling,* "of innumerable solid particles separated one from another," which composed the secondary tail, was, by reason of the intense heat, separated from the nucleus or head of the comet, it was projected into space with increased and constantly increasing velocity due to its nearer approach to the sun. Hence, when near the perihelion change of direction the tail would seem to be driven back upon the nucleus.

" Considerable discussion has taken place as to the origin of the spectrum seen at the base of a candle or gas flame. At first, observation seemed to point to the fact that it was due to a hydrocarbon. It has been ascertained, however, that sparks taken in cyanogen gas, even when dried

* Spectrum Analysis, p. 568.

with all care, show the spectrum, and a flame of cyanogen and oxygen gives the same bands brilliantly. These facts have convinced the majority of observers that the spectrum is a *true carbon spectrum*."*

Prof. Tyndall has made us acquainted, not only with the peculiar properties and the marvellous distribution of aqueous vapor, but also of the most infinitesimal dust-particles that so thoroughly permeate our atmosphere, and are made manifest when it is agitated or disturbed. These particles are utterly impalpable, and are only made visible in sunbeams. Their existence may be made manifest in an extraordinary manner by means of the blue flame. We have noticed the brilliancy of the field when charged with finely comminuted charcoal, lodestone or iron.

To vary the experiment we resorted to friction, rubbing briskly the brass tube or wick of a common Bunsen burner with a two-pound lodestone, the ventilator in the bottom of the tube being left entirely open so that only the blue carbon flame escaped from the top. Immediately bright conical streaks appeared in the flame, intermittent and disappearing when the friction ceased. By substituting raps- for friction the brilliancy of the whole flame was greatly increased and its volume slightly enlarged. For the moment the result was startling since it seemed to show that magnetism

* Art. Spectroscopy, Cyc. Brit., 19th Edition.

SPECTRUM OF GAS FLAME. 151

was matter that was being consumed by the carbon flame. But continuing and varying the experiment, it was found that rubbing or rapping the tube with any solid substance would produce the same effect, much less forcibly, however, with friction than with rapping. Another singular effect was, that by rapping the rubber tube that conveyed the gas into the Bunsen wick, at a little distance from the base of the burner a similar but less continuous and brilliant effect was manifest.

Projecting moisture into the flame by the elastic force of a damp tooth-brush rubbed across the fingers also increased the brilliancy of the whole volume of flame. This shows that water, when first projected into a burning building, adds fuel to the flame. When the heat is sufficiently intense to convert the water into steam the flame is extinguished.

Every person who has used a clothes or hair brush knows that after use, by rubbing them across the fingers or any other substance, particles of dust and other visible matter are expelled from them. After these particles have ceased to be visible, turn the brushes toward the carbon flame and rub them as before. The brilliancy of the flame is at once increased. Rub one piece of iron quickly across another towards the flame. A most brilliant flame is exhibited. Rub a stiff tooth-brush across the flat surface of a lodestone towards the flame. A still more brilliant flame filled with incandescent sparks will rush up from the tube. We had made a steel tube or wick to fit an ordinary Bunsen burner and repeated these experiments with it, in some cases with more brilliant effect than with the brass tube. The steel was necessarily magnetized both by friction and rapping during the experiments. With both the brass and steel tubes, by scraping off particles of lodestone on the upper edge so that they came in contact with the flame, a yellowish green color appeared at the base of the flame from the brass tube which we attributed to the copper in its composition, but a bright green appeared at the base of the flame from the steel tube, which the spectroscope may show to be the spectrum of the lodestone flame. With a slightly moistened tooth-brush take up some floured lodestone that has been sifted through flannel and project it into the flame. A scintillating blaze of glory will be the result. After handling lodestones, iron, charcoal and other substances, brush the fingers of the right hand briskly across those of the left and toward the flame; it will become more brilliant intermittingly, and incandescent sparks will appear.

As there can be no combustion except through the agency of matter, whence comes the matter that illumines the carbon flame? We can trace that from the water, the iron, the lodestone, the charcoal, and the particles of dust. But whence comes that from the flesh of the hands? Since flame is incontestibly the product of the combustion of matter, how infinitely infinitesimal, in this case, must be the particles of that matter? Is it possible that the ether can be more ethereal than this? If not, the resistless logic of the question seems to be that *ether is matter.* Another argument in favor of the same conclusion may be cited. We know that nothing but matter except magnetism can resist matter in motion. In a perfect vacuum all substances light or heavy, fall with the same velocity. In the atmosphere they fall with unequal velocities, the feather less rapidly than the leaden bullet. Now it is held that the ether resists the motion of the planets in their orbits and at the same time helps to support them as they revolve on their axes. If this argument is sound it is a further indication that ether is matter.

A very good illustration of the above conditions is furnished by the flame of a Bunsen gas-burner when the ventilator at the bottom of the tube is left entirely open so that the air may be admitted to the lower part of the flame. The faint fringe of light that borders the outer and upper edge of the flame produced by the combustion of the oxygen from the air with a slight portion of hydrogen, represents the coma; the denser yellow flame produced by the combustion of the " solid bodies," both of the gas and such as may escape from the inner surface of the tube, represents the nucleus, and the beautifully transparent slightly blue flame that immediately follows is the carbon flame that forms the tails of comets.

To illustrate this more effectually we prepared a single tube or metallic wick to receive the gas from two Bunsen burners. The orifice for the escape of the concentrated flame of both burners was three inches wide. When the gas was turned on full head with the ventilators entirely open we had a splendid jet of flame three inches wide and about eight inches high at the centre of the flame arch. We thus had a curtain of light-blue transparent flame equal to a parallelogram about three inches wide and four inches high.

With a glass blow-pipe we sent a current of air through the curtain. The heat was carried beyond arm's length. With a small nozzle attached to the rubber tube of an air-pump, and turning on a strong current of air a conical volume of heat was developed, the heat being quite strong at its apex near the blue curtain, and detected by the hand some twelve to fifteen feet distant. Counter-currents from any source should be excluded.

When the Bunsen flame was ascending undisturbed, a fine effect was produced by sprinkling or ejecting into it finely comminuted particles of any metal or mineral. Particles of carbon gave a profusion of brilliant sparks. Thoroughly pulverized lodestone and iron yielded copious volumes of bright flame. If this be a true synthesis of comet's tails, then every lighted candle and gas-flame has been manufacturing them for centuries past.

Says Sir John Herschel, "The constitution of the nubeculæ—the Magellanic clouds—especially that of nubecula major, is found to be of astonishing complexity. The general ground of both consists of large tracts and patches of nebulosity in every stage of resolution, . . . nebulæ in abundance both regular and irregular; globular clusters in every state of condensation; and objects of a nebulous character quite peculiar, and which have no analogue in any other region of the heavens." These objects of a nebulous character may possibly be masses of glowing gas similar to those discovered by Huggins in the nebula of Draco. Whatever may be their constitution they appear to be permanently fixed in the far south-eastern portion of the heavens.

Remembering that by our hypothesis there are several stellar systems in each of the hyperboloids, we may assume that two of these systems are adjacent to each other in two adjoining hyperboloids, but not in the same latitude, so to speak, in space, and that they are also within telescopic reach of each other. Let us further assume that the system to which our earth belongs is within telescopic reach of the system that lies next east of it. We know that our telescopes reveal to us many celestial bodies lying far beyond the planets connected with our system, that many of these bodies are suns, and that each sun is supposed to be the centre of another system. All these bodies revolve in the same general direction. Hence it may happen that, from our earth, moving along the *eastern* side of our system, we may, with the aid of the telescope, observe the celestial bodies moving—or rather existing, for they can hardly be said to move—in the *western* side of the neighboring system. The Magellanic clouds may belong to this neighboring system and be at an immense distance from their primary in the direction of our primary, and so within reach of our telescopes. This seems to be a satisfactory explanation of their position.

The eccentric motions of the stars in the celestial vault may also be satisfactorily explained by our hypothesis. While the stars are all moving in one general direction some of them appear to be moving in opposite directions. This may be shown by the two supposed neighboring systems. Place two celestial globes of equal size side by side with their axes horizontal, parallel and standing north and south. Note a star on the meridian of one of the globes and another star on the opposite side of the meridian of the other globe.

Now, rotate both globes from west to east. While the first star *sinks* to its horizon the other star will *rise* to its horizon, and then as they continue to revolve they will appear to be moving in opposite directions. By destroying the parallelism of their axes an obliquity of rotation will be apparent. In like manner we may suppose the telescope will reveal to our view other stars of different magnitudes belonging to other neighboring systems. The inclination of their axes of rotation may greatly vary and every kind of motion be exhibited.

We may here notice a peculiar optical illusion connected with the motion of double stars. Imagine two stars of any magnitude made easily visible by our telescopes, to be so situated in space as to be nearly in range with each other, and suppose their rotary motion to be in the same direction, but with *different velocities*. Under these conditions the two stars will appear to be moving in opposite directions, the star that moves slowest appearing to move in a direction contrary to that of the other. If the spectator could have a lateral view of the pair, he would recognize the immense distance between them.

XX.

The Age of the Earth.

WE are less interested in what may be the age of the earth at the present time, than we are in what may be its future term of existence. Some authorities suppose it to have existed about ten millions of years and that it may possibly continue to exist for about eighteen millions more. Its future life depends, primarily, on the heat derived from the sun and secondarily on what Helmholtz calls certain "physico-mechanical laws."

Every decrease in the temperature of the sun is followed, ultimately, by a decrease in the temperature of the interior of the earth. When this temperature reaches a point so low that the earth's surface will not support vegetable life then all life, both vegetable and animal, will cease to exist. The operation of the tides and winds, the resistance resulting from the inequalities in the depth of the oceans and seas and the elevation of mountains are mechanical forces which, it is claimed, will slowly but surely retard the rotary motion of the planet, and finally reduce it to a condition of utter barrenness and desolation. Laplace, however, says: * "The currents of the sea, the rivers, earthquakes and winds do not alter the rotation of the earth," and also that "For the last 2000 years the sun's mass has not varied the two millionth part." †

Under our hypothesis a very different result may be anticipated. That hypothesis provides an abundant and constant supply of fuel for all suns in the future. We know that our sun is rated as a star of about the 4th magnitude. There are a great number of stars in the firmament of vastly greater size and intenser brightness. We have before referred to Alpha Centauri, Sirius and Capella. Our sun would cast a shadow on either of them if placed between the two with Sirius serving as a screen. We also know that the stars vary in intrinsic brightness as well as in size.

Now, in view of the infinite supply of fuel poured into the stellar systems from outer space we may legitimately assume that all suns may increase in size and also in intrinsic brightness and calorific force. Hence it may follow that no planet will ever perish from diminution of the heat-supply, but, on the contrary, may melt with fervent heat or be destroyed by the operation of "physico-mechanical laws." Indeed we may with reason-

* Mec. Cel. Vol. II., Book V., Bowditch's Translation.
† Id. Vol. IV., p. 622.

able confidence believe that, from this cause, all planets will ultimately cease to exist as planets and that their elements may be transformed into other ponderables and imponderables that may furnish fuel for distant suns or supply material for new planets to revolve in other spheres.

Suns also, may wax and wane and perish and be resurgent in other suns. But there is no necessity that they should do so, since there is never a lack of fuel for their flame. There may be variation in the intensity of their radiance and calorescence as the proportions of hydrogen, oxygen and carbon or nitrogen and ammonia may vary in the fuel supplied.

XXI.

The Sun and the Aurora.

THAT we may better understand the character of the fixed stars, all of which are supposed to be suns, we may briefly study that of our own. The generally accepted theory of its constitution is that its centre is composed of partially if not wholly liquified solids, of which the spectroscope has revealed the following: iron, nickel, copper, zinc, sulphur, and indeed, most of the substances of which the crust of our earth is composed; that these are surrounded by the photosphere or visible surface of the sun, a kind of dense atmosphere composed of clouds formed by the combination and condensation of such of the solar gases as are sufficiently cooled off by their radiation into space. Outside of the photosphere, is the chromosphere, a layer of uncondensed gas which overlies it. The lower portion of the chromosphere is rich in all the vapors and gases which enter into the sun's composition.

At a comparatively small elevation the heavier

gases disappear, giving place to the lighter gases, especially to hydrogen which extends beyond the surface of the sun to immense distances in every direction. Certain highly-colored prominences originating, apparently, in the chromosphere are considered by Young to be extensions of it projected upward to great altitudes and forming enormous clouds as beautiful, variable and changeable as those which we see in our terrestrial sky.

Proctor, discussing the corona and the observed association between these colored prominences and the inner and brighter parts of the corona says: " That in some way or other electricity is at work in the production of the coronal light, may well be believed; and further, that electrical action is at work in some special manner above the prominence regions is far from impossible." *

There is a difference of opinion as to the origin of the spots on the sun. We do not discuss this question since, for our purposes, we are only interested in knowing that a close correlation has been proved to exist between them and the earth's magnetism. The magnetic needle responds to their influence as readily and distinctly as it does to that of the aurora. The observations of Ångström and Respighi showed that the aurora and the zodiacal light are identical. The more rapid the motion of the rays or streamers of the aurora the greater is the excitement of the magnetic needle.

* Orbs Around Us, pp. 276-278.

In his monograph on the Auroræ Mr. J. Rand Capron mentions one observed in 1877 by Mr. Carl Bork, a Norwegian naturalist, and painted by him from nature, in oil colors. The painting is remarkable for the distinct but tender green of some of the streamers.

It is claimed that the spectroscopic observations of the zodiacal light made by Ångström from which he concluded that it developed the same green line that is exhibited in the aurora, are not verified by later observations. But if the zodiacal light and the aurora are identical as claimed by him and Respighi, then there is conclusive reason to believe that their spectra are identical. And the probability is that if the vibrations or undulations of the zodiacal light were as rapid as those of the aurora, the green line would be distinctly developed in it.

XXII.

The Age of the Stars.

It will be remembered that Sir William Herschel was the first to suggest that the nebulæ may furnish us an indication of the *age* of the stars. This idea is repeated and more or less elaborated by Father Secchi, Prof. Tait and Prof. Langley; by the first very slightly, by the two latter more fully. Says Father Secchi, "It is not very long since it was believed that the stellar spaces were peopled only by well-defined and compact bodies; now there have been discovered those enormous masses of gas which are, perhaps, destined to constitute other solid bodies, if even already there are not some of them *solidified*, of which light has not yet brought us the announcement."

Prof. Tait,[*] commenting on Fourier's great work on "Heat Conduction" says: "In astronomy it leads us to the grand question of the age, or perhaps more correctly of the *phase of life* of a star or a nebulæ; shows us the material of potential

[*] Recent Advances in Physical Science, p. 22.

suns, other suns in the process of formation, in vigorous youth and in every stage of protracted decay. It leads us to look on each planet and satellite as having been at one time a tiny sun, a member of some binary or multiple group, and even now presenting an endless variety of subjects for the application of its methods. It leads us forward in thought, to the far distant time when the materials of the present stellar systems shall have lost all but their mutual potential energy, but shall in virtue of it form the materials of further larger suns with their attendant planets."

Prof. Langley,* concerning the developments of the spectroscope says: " Again, in showing us the composition of the stars it has also shown us more, for it has enabled us to form a conjecture as to the relative ages of the stars and suns," and of the different features and characteristics of the stars, " that a succession in age is not improbably pointed at in these types. Yet if we admit this temperature classification of the stars, we are not far from admitting that the spectroscope is now pointing out the stages in the life of suns themselves; suns just beginning their life of almost infinite years; suns in the middle of their course; suns which are growing old and casting feebler beams."

* New Astronomy, p. 238.

XXIII.

The Southern Hemisphere and the Magellanic Clouds.

WE have stated (*supra*) that Sir William Herschel was the first to emphasize the fact that the southern hemisphere is much less rich in the number and magnitude of its stars than the northern. But it is richest in nubeculæ and nebulæ. To Sir William and Sir John Herschel we are mostly indebted for our knowledge of the marvellous beauty and wonderful character of the nubeculæ, the Magellanic clouds.

" The constitution," says Sir John, " of the nubecula, and especially of the nubecula major, is found to be of astonishing complexity. The general ground of both consists of large tracts and patches of nebulosity in every stage of resolution, from light irresolvable with eighteen inches of reflecting aperture, up to perfectly separated stars like the milky way, and clustering groups sufficiently insulated and condensed to come under the designation of irregular, and in some cases, pretty rich clusters. But besides those there are also nebulæ in abundance both regular and irregular; globular clusters in every state of condensation; and objects of a nebulous character quite peculiar, and which have no analogue in any other region of the heavens."

Speaking of the *glory* of portions of the southern sky, Dr. A. B. Gould * says, *that* " in the region of the southern cross is indescribable. There where the milky way is crossed by the thick stream of bright stars which skirts the rim of light, its brilliancy is wonderfully increased, and it exhibits a magnificence unequalled in any other portion of the heavens."

Humboldt writes that the lesser of the Magellanic clouds "is surrounded with a kind of desert, a desert of intensest darkness." We shall notice in the sequel the significance of the position and composition of these clouds.

Swedenborg was first to note, in 1734, the variation of the magnetic force from the equator to the poles, a fact afterward noted by La Perouse, in 1787, and still later by Humboldt, in 1798. " The intensity of this force," says Humboldt, " is least at the equator and greatest at the poles."

Swedenborg also noted the fact that the southern magnetic axis is longer than the northern, a fact also noted by Prof. Hansteen, in 1819, and confirmed by Sir James Ross during the cruise of the Erebus and Terror, in 1839-1843. It is one of the most interesting phenomena connected with the

* Account of the Cordoba Observatory.

motion of our globe. The position of the two poles is given as follows:

South magnetic pole 75° 5' South Lat.

North magnetic pole 75° 0' North Lat.

Prof. Hansteen gives the following: Period of revolution of North Mag. pole, 1890 years, mean annual motion 11'425. Period of revolution of South Mag. pole, 4605 years, mean annual motion 4'69.

Discussing the investigations of Sabine, Ross and Gauss, Humboldt writes,[*] "if the intensity near the south magnetic pole be expressed by 2.052, Sabine found it was only 1.624 at the North Mag. pole." Sir Isaac Newton proved that the precession of the equinoxes was due to the preponderance of matter about the earth's equator as compared with its poles, whereby the former was more strongly attracted than the latter, thus producing a gyratory or wabbling motion of the poles of the earth around those of the ecliptic.

If the fact that the southern magnetic axis is longer than the northern shows that the centre of gravity in the earth is not the centre of figure, this latter lying nearest to the north pole, then this fact would materially influence the precession of the equinox.

[*] Kosmos, Vol. I. p. 197.

XXIV.

A New Cosmography and Celestial Geography.

It remains for us to apply the facts and forces we have been considering to the Geography of the Heavens, the distribution and motions of the stars, the system or systems under which they are arranged and the laws which govern their movements and influence their duration. Following Bacon and Kant who, as before noted, designated Time and Space as "Forms," we have assigned certain Forms to space in developing the new cosmography and the new celestial geography.

There are two ideas, or rather beliefs, that are strongly intrenched in the popular mind. One is that the stars are infinite in number and another is that they are infinite in duration, that they will never die. We shall learn that they are not infinite in number and that all the planetary stars may cease to exist.

There are certain curves and surfaces that we shall need to utilize and refer to so frequently that it will be well to understand their origin, forms and functions. All these curves, and none others, can be cut from a single right-angled cone. If we pass a plane through this cone perpendicular to its axis it will cut out a circle; if we pass it at any angle with the axis greater than 45° it will cut out an ellipse; if parallel to the axis at any distance below the apex, an hyperbola; if parallel to the side, a parabola.

If the plane be passed from the apex to the base along the axis, it will cut out an isosceles triangle. If we revolve a circle upon either of its diameters it will generate a sphere; if we revolve an ellipse on either of its axes it will generate an ellipsoid; if we revolve a parabola upon its major axis it will generate a paraboloid and if we revolve an hyperbola upon its major axis it will generate an hyperboloid.

These curves have certain characteristics. A circular space or area is the largest that can be enclosed by any given line. The planets rotate on their axes in circles, they revolve in their orbits in ellipses. Periodical comets revolve round the sun in ellipses; unreturning comets in parabolic or hyperbolic curves. The trajectories of shooting stars are parabolic.

In a solid cube of wood we can cut out or excavate an hyperboloid from each of its sides. The straight lines joining the centres of each pair of opposite sides will pass through the centre of the cube itself and will form the major axes of the hyperboloids.

The two hyperboloids opposite each other and having a common axis are technically called nappes.

As there are six hyperboloids there will be three pair of nappes. The straight lines passing at right angles to each other, through the point of intersection of the two major axes of the nappes and tangent to the curve or surface at an infinite distance, are called asymptotes. The hyperbolic curve and the right line called the asymptote or tangent, bear a peculiar relation to each other for, although the latter is called tangent to the former, yet, practically, they never coincide, as is mathematically demonstrated.* The spaces, cut out of our cube, which form the hyperboloids are hyperboloidal spaces. The space between the hyperboloids but exterior to them is an asymptotic space. For convenience we may call it an asymptoid.

Now, concerning all these lines and spaces we notice one transcendent truth, that, as here combined, they all have their origin in one common centre and they are all infinite in extent.

If a sun possessing infinite photometric power were placed at that centre its rays, if they met with no obstruction, would illuminate all space.

If infinite space were illuminated by a vast number

---

* Upon this fact is founded Addison's famous comparison of the spirit of man with the Divine spirit. (*Spectator* No. III.) "The soul," he says, "considered with its Creator, is like one of those mathematical lines that may draw nearer to another for all eternity without a possibility of touching it."

of suns attended by their secondary orbs, an allseeing eye, placed at that centre could survey and scan them all.

If an omnipotent, inherent, self-acting force were placed at that centre it could sway, move, govern them all.

XXV.

The New System.—The Asymptoid and the Hyperboloids.—The Matter and Motion Within Them.

ALL philosophers and astronomers have supposed space to be filled with matter which is, in part, systematically arranged, is subjected to certain forces and governed by certain laws, but no specific, original form in which it exists and is conserved until needed for use in organic work has been proposed. As we have already stated, the stellar system that meets with most favor and is generally accepted as true, is that which is based upon the nebular hypothesis. The culmination of this system is the Milky Way accompanied by star clusters, young stars, nubeculæ, nebulæ and star-dust.

Its most sublime and striking features have been described and mapped by the Herschels and by Father Secchi. A small section of it in which our sun is supposed to be located has been especially delineated. This system is very grand and impressive, but how small a portion, comparatively, of infinite space does it utilize, does it occupy?

The only system which transcends this, which sweeps into wider areas and recognizes other Milky Ways with all their grand accompaniments is that of Lambert, which has been already noticed.

The new system it is proposed to develop begins with the hypothesis that all space, by the action of certain laws, is divided into different forms or compartments in the manner we have already indicated; that the chief central form to which all the others adjoin is the asymptotic which we call the asymptoid; that this spreads out infinitely and embraces, but does not surround, the six hyperboloidal forms or spaces which we designate as hyperboloids. These six forms, as before noted constitute three pairs of nappes. All the nappes extend outward infinitely from the lines in which they adjoin the asymptoid. The axes of these nappes intersect each other at right angles and are infinite in length. This point of intersection is the apex of the cone from which the hyperboloids were cut. These hyperboloids are all exactly equal to each other and, mathematically, their equations are identical.

The points at which the axes of the nappes intersect the hyperboloids are in the centre of the hyperboloids themselves, and the positive poles of all the suns in all the hyperboloids also point towards this centre, as the positive poles in all the planets point towards their suns. All the planets connected with all the suns in all the hyperboloids

South.

The X-shaped space represents the Asymptoid with Spheres. The other spaces are parts of yperboloids with Planets, etc.

E. The Earth.
M. The Magellanic Clouds.
AA. Asymptotes.

THE NEW SYSTEM.   175

revolve from west to east or from left to right, and possibly the whole omniverse may revolve in the same direction.

We speak of "fixed stars." They are so approximately in size and in intrinsic brightness and in relation to each other. But since the planets have a circular rotation on their axes and revolve in ellipses around their primaries, in both cases with vastly different velocities and in vastly different times, it is evident that not one of them occupies the same position in space during any two consecutive periods of time nor will any of them hereafter occupy any position that they have occupied heretofore. Motion is the life of stars, stagnation their death. We must emphasize the cardinal fact that the arms, so to designate them, of the asymptoid grow constantly narrower as they recede from the vertex of the curve or form.

The hyperboloids are six domes. The areas of these domes are constantly enlarged as their axes are more and more elongated. Considering them as spaces occupied by celestial bodies it seems clear that light must diminish as it recedes from their centres until it is lost in the utter darkness that envelops them all.

Some of the gases after their formation under fixed laws as before noted which have strong affinities for each other may be combined in their partially condensed condition. Other and innumerable combinations, adhesions and mechanical associations may occur between them in all stages between the extreme poles. And by these varied and numberless combinations every possible form and kind of matter is produced. Hence we have stellar and planetary systems with all their accompaniments and belongings; suns of every size and kind and color; planets, large and small, with or without a single or several satellites; asteroids, meteorites, star clusters, nebulæ, nubeculæ and star-dust. To the omnipresence of magnetism we must add its omnipotence, in the sense of its infinite and constant action, its persistent, pervasive *vis-viva*. It is always alive. There are various and simple ways of showing this. The simplest is the single thermo-electric pair formed by uniting bars of antimony and bismuth at one end and connecting the opposite, open ends, with a wire. By heating the united ends a direct current will be generated; by cooling them the current will be reversed.

Another simple method of exhibiting the magnetic force is the following. Place a magnetic needle in its normal condition when at rest standing north and south. From a distance outside, at right angles to the needle, present to it the poles of a magnet. As like poles repel and unlike poles attract, let us use the north pole of the needle and of the magnet. As we approach the magnet to the needle from the east the latter is deflected to the west. It is pushed out of its normal direction more and more the nearer the magnet approaches

THE NEW SYSTEM. 177

it. This pushing is persistent so long as the relative positions of the magnet and the needle are maintained. From month to month, year to year, these opposite forces will continue to act. With the least variation in the intensity of the magnetism either in the atmosphere or the magnet, motion is instantly manifested.

It is not simply inertia, it is in fact a perpetual force and also practically, perpetual motion, for the invisible vibrations of force are constantly passing between the magnet and the needle, manifest motion resulting, as we have stated, the moment there is any variation in the magnetic tension.

"In the incandescent points which produce the electric light, when the current is turned off darkness ensues, but they do not cease to radiate. There is still a copious emission from the points." *

It has been shown by Matteucci that, in living animals an electric current is perpetually circulating between the external and internal portions of the muscles. If the physical elements of the body were imperishable and unchangeable, this motion would be perpetual.

Any number of needles may be placed in the line of magnetic action and all of them will be more or less deflected according to their distance from the magnet. We placed four needles in this line, the first needle one inch, the second two, the third three and the fourth six inches long, which

* Tyndall: Heat as Motion, § 306.

we designated in the same order as Mercury, Venus, the Earth and Mars. They were placed at distances from the magnet varying from 12 to 60 inches, the longest needle at the greatest distance.

The removal of the three interior needles from the line of force did not cause the slightest variation in the deflection of the outer one. As many needles, of any length, as the space would hold, could be placed in the line of magnetic force, and each would at once be deflected to the same extent that it would when it stood alone in the line, each needle contributing its own latent magnetism to the main line of force. It is this magnetic force, as we have indicated, that determines the conditions and motions of the matter in the hyperboloids. The next question is one of intense interest, namely: what are the contents of the asymptoid and to what conditions and motions are they subjected? Difficult as the question is we do not despair of its partial elucidation.

Let us again note more particularly the form and position of this space in reference to all space. We have already described its geometrical origin and figure, showing that it holds within its embracing but not surrounding curve as before stated, six exactly equal and homogeneous hyperboloids. Hence its centre may, for our purpose, be considered as the centre of all space, since every radius extending outward from that centre will be infinite. We have also pointed out the wonderful characteristics of this centre, the perfect equilibrium of all space and matter around it and that from it, every adequate influence, energy or force could be easily, equably and systematically distributed and extended in all possible directions. We have also noted the origin—Deity—of all power, energy and force. We may then consider this asymptotic space, from its peculiar and absolutely central position and its marvellous adaptability for the propagation of infinite action, to be the seat of infinite power or, as we may reverently suggest, the dwelling-place of God.

XXVI.

The Asymptoid.—Transcendental Matter.—Light without Heat.—Peculiar Function of Nitrogen.—Nitrogen Zones.—Exhilarating Atmosphere.—Radiant Matter.

WHAT are the contents of this space? We may reach some conclusions concerning them by analogy, by inference from what we know of those appertaining to the hyperboidal spaces. We have studied the character and properties of the various forms of matter which they contain, of the ponderables and imponderables, and of the various forces to which they are subjected. All this matter and all these forces are very substantial, very real and easily and effectively made manifest to our senses. It appears reasonable to infer that they must be analogous to those found in the asymptoid.

But we may readily believe that the latter are of a more transcendental character. We know that matter exists here in an almost infinite variety of forms, and that some kinds of matter are allotropic, that they are capable of existing in two or more conditions which are distinct in their physi-

THE ASYMPTOID. 181

cal or chemical relations. The most familiar and conspicuous of these is carbon, which occurs crystallized in octahedrons and other related forms, in a state of extreme hardness in the diamond; it also occurs in hexagonal forms of little hardness, as black lead, and again in a third form of entire softness as lampblack and charcoal. In some cases one of the allotropics is peculiarly an active state and the other a passive one. Thus, among gases, ozone is an active state of oxygen and is distinct from ordinary oxygen which is the element in its passive state.

There are several other substances that exist under conditions that are, chemically, quite distinct though not exactly allotropic. We also know that the spectroscope reveals to us in all the celestial bodies numerous forms of matter that are identical with those that we find in our own solar system. We may, therefore, legitimately conclude that entirely similar forms of matter exist within the asymptoid, and that they may be more eclectic, more transcendental in their properties and characteristics, that they may be less dense, more refined, more delicate in their structure. And the illuminating and calorific conditions of the asymptoid may be as transcendental as its matter.

"The sole difference," says Tyndall, "between light and radiant heat is one of period. The waves of the one are short and of rapid occurrence, while the waves of the other are long and of slow occurrence." From the refinement and exaltation of everything pertaining to the asymptoid we may infer that the light and heat developed within it must be of the same character. That light will be, not sparkling, intermittent, dazzling, but the calm, steady, transcendent, eternal glow of the Light Ineffable; the heat, not intense, scorching, oppressive, but gentle, radiant, glowing, illustrating, in its supremest state, that peculiar condition of light without heat of which nature furnishes us miniature examples in the firefly—Lamphyridæ—and the glowworm—Elateridæ.

These two lights are a most interesting study. They are, considering the size of the living, fleshly forms in which they are developed, as brilliant as that of suns. When caught and held in the hand no sensation of heat is felt, whereas if a person held in the same way two bits of charcoal of the same size heated to redness, the burn would be most painful.

The experiments of Mr. N. Tesla as reported in a lecture before the Electrical Engineers in London, show decided progress in the development of this kind of light. We may also mention his very sanguine expectation, twice expressed, that under certain conditions "telephoning could be rendered practicable across the Atlantic" and also that "ere many generations pass our machinery will be a power obtainable at any point in the universe. . . . . Throughout all space there is energy. Is this energy static or kinetic ? If static, our hopes are in vain ; if kinetic, and this we know it is for certain, then it is a mere question of time when men will succeed in attaching their machinery to the very wheelwork of nature."

The advice of the late Mr. R. Waldo Emerson was "hitch your wagon to the star." Mr. Tesla apparently expects to accomplish this end by the aid of electric traces. However, it has been abundantly demonstrated by modern hypnotists that Telepathy—thought transference, thought exchange—is practicable through thousands of miles and there is no reason to doubt that it may be achieved through much greater distances. Answered silent prayer is successful Telepathy, whatever the distance necessary to secure that success may be.

The gases, refined and purified, must be found in the asymptoid. The four most important of these are oxygen, hydrogen, nitrogen and carbonic acid. The three first are electric conductors, the more dense the more effective. Carbon, as we have seen, is a good conductor in all its forms except the diamond.

Nitrogen is devoid of color, taste or smell, is mechanically mixed with oxygen in our atmosphere and combined with it in nitrous oxide. Whereas oxygen is the most magnetic of all the gases, nitrogen is not at all so, it is entirely neutral or zero.

Another remarkable property is its power to sustain life, which indeed cannot be continuously sustained without it. It not merely helps to sustain life but under certain conditions, as we have before noted, produces its highest exaltation. Strangely antagonistic to this is its destructive, explosive power. It is an indispensable ingredient in the different forms of gunpowder and dynamite, is supposed to be, and undoubtedly is effective in the explosion of thunderbolts.

Another of its marked peculiarities is its partial opacity to heat and transparency to light. While it permits the transmission of the radiant light of the asymptoid into the hyperboloids it partially absorbs the oppressive heat of the latter and prevents its passage into the former.

Ammonia is composed of one part of nitrogen and two of hydrogen. Now hydrochlorate, carbonate and sulphate of ammonia absorb heat and extinguish combustion according to their density. Leslie proved that heated bodies cool more rapidly in hydrogen gas than in our atmosphere, and Tyndall showed that a continuous spectrum of nitrous acid gas thrown on a screen developed, under certain conditions, numerous dark bands, the rays of which are intercepted by the gas while the intervening bands of light were allowed to pass.

At this point we call especial attention to a peculiar function of nitrogen as connected, by our hypothesis, with the forms and divisions of the new system. We know that of the three so called permaent gases, oxygen, nitrogen and hydrogen, the specific gravity of the first is greatest, of nitrogen next, while hydrogen is lightest. As we ascend from planets into space these gases occur in the same order, the heaviest gas, under normal conditions, being always lowest.

We have supposed that all the forms of matter and force, all things within the asymptoid are more eclectic, more transcendental than the forms of matter and force and all things in the hyperboloids. Hence there needs be something to indicate the space which separates them, that lies between them. Now nitrogen, magnetically, is zero, neutral, neither attractive nor repulsive, while at the same time it may be thoroughly and easily permeated by the magnetic force. It also, as we have noted, transmits light and absorbs heat.

With these peculiar and remarkable properties it is admirably fitted for a dividing curtain between the asymptoid and the hyperboloids. And that is the function we may suppose the nitrogen to exhibit, and, therefore, that a zone of gases of which nitrogen is the chief constituent, ammonia being another, fringes each of the hyperboloids.

As oxygen is the most abundant and indispensable of the gases in the hyperboloids so in its eclectic state it must be most effective and pervasive in the asymptoid, and the oxygen and nitrogen which here form exhilarating gas may there be so refined, so transformed, and so exquisitely combined as to form an atmosphere, the mere respiration of which will be a perpetual delight.

As indicating the *extent* rather than the *character* of the difference between the forms of matter in the asymptoid and the hyperboloids it may be suggested that the granite of that space may be diamond; and the gems may all be transfigured; the flowers may be the shadowy embodiment of a perfume; the water, flowing volumes of radiant mist, and its bow of promise a transfigured iris. All good and beautiful things we know here may be transfigured and glorified there.

And we may the more reasonably anticipate results similar to these when we study the beautiful experiments of Crooke with "radiant matter" operating in vacuum tubes or bulbs of glass, particularly the delicate shadow of the cross, the fanciful glass railway and the fairy-like wind-mill of the radiometer, heretofore noticed. It will be borne in mind that these tubes do not furnish a perfect vacuum.

XXVII.

Spirits.—Spiritism.—Magnetism in the Inner and Outer-stellar Space.—The Ether, What is it? —New Matter.—Creation and Evolution.

DEFINING *Spirit* as the highest order of wisdom, of consciousness, we may define spiritism as the action of spirit on matter in a manner analogous to the action of thought on the brain or of the will on the muscles.

In certain cases, " when we come to electricity," says Dr. Lodge,* " we find that some kind of matter has more electricity associated with it than others, so that for a given electromotive force we get a greater electric displacement; that the electricity is, as it were, denser in some kinds of matter than in others." We have shown (on p. 18) that magnetism can be condensed, compressed, and that, under certain conditions, what Faraday calls "physical lines of magnetic force," must be considered as extending to an infinite distance. We know that magnetism can also be expanded.

* Modern Views of Electricity, p. 349.

Hence the magnetism of the asymptoid may be less condensed than that in the hyperboloids, to which, however, it must respond.

We must further note that there are at the present time a certain limited number of solar systems containing a limited number of celestial bodies. Were there ever a greater number of these systems and bodies? Whatever may have been true in the past we know that, by the law of the conservation of forces and the indestructibility of matter, whatever changes there may have been in the number and condition of these systems and bodies there can never be any less or greater amount of force, nor any less or greater quantity of matter in them than now. These forces and this quantity of matter may be sufficient to sustain the present systems indefinitely in their numerous and varied changes.

But it is impossible that they should furnish matter for any new systems. It is equally impossible to believe that the work of creation or evolution is ended; that no more radiant suns are to illumine the outer darkness; that no other planets are to respond to their genial influence; that the boundless realms of outer-space are to be shrouded in the blackness of darkness forever; that the work of Deity is finished, and that God is henceforth to rest content in the contemplation of a completed task, or rather in the suspension of the exercise of His omnipotent will.

SPIRITISM, NEW MATTER. 189

Whence, then, is to be drawn the new matter for new worlds? From the outer-stellar space. This infinite outer-stellar space is a reservoir containing an infinite supply of matter for an infinite number of solar systems. Since all matter is amenable to the magnetic force the latter becomes a carrier for the former, endless quantities of which it transports into the hyperboloids where it is transformed into all varieties of celestial bodies. The first form of transformation is "star-dust" or "world-stuff." As the magnetic force increases in strength the succeeding forms are the nubeculæ, nebulæ, meteorites, comets, asteroids, planets and suns. These are constantly forming, growing, grouping according to the laws by which they are governed. While these laws are certain and persistent they are at the same time elastic, flexible, accommodating in their action. No forces nor forms of matter in any one hyperboloid can interfere with or derange the forces or forms of matter in any other hyperboloid. Every celestial body must revolve or move within the limits of the space in which it originated.

Hence, by our hypothesis the illimitable stores of the outer-stellar space are constantly poured into the limited zones of the hyperboloids. Hence again, we have inexhaustible fuel for perpetual consumption, and hence also, we have in all the stellar and planetary systems the most perfect, the most sublime exhibition of perpetual motion. The system is complete. All its forms are homogeneous, harmonious. Its equilibrium is absolutely perfect. Its mechanism it seems impossible to improve. Its action is smooth, direct, orderly and systematic. Under it the grand processes of nature are carried forward and developed without haste and without hesitation, but with unerring purpose and absolute certainty. And it is automatic, self-supporting, self-sustaining. Neither its matter, its motion, or its force, or energy can be annihilated. And yet this grand system, admitting its actual existence, is as absolutely a creation as would be that of a single planet or a single organism. It is quite immaterial whether the ultimate end of that creation be consummated in six days or six millions of years. It is the result of a law established by an Infinite Power, an Infinite Will, and to such a Will, such a Power, instantaneous production is as easy as the most protracted period of evolution.

We may here repeat our hypothesis concerning the origin, genesis and operation of all possible forms of energy. While it is no part of our design to discuss theological or teleological questions, it seems necessary here to consider one point relating to Deity. The popular idea of God is that his chief attributes are omniscience, omnipotence and omnipresence. As to the latter, the Rev. Theodore Parker's characterization of it may be considered a fair expression of the popular no-tion. In one of his "Ten Sermons of Religion," he says: "God must be omnipresent in space. There can be no mote that peoples the sunbeams, no spot on an insect's wing, no little cell of life which the microscope discovers in the seed-sproule of a moss and brings to light, but God is there, in that mote, in that spot, in that cell."

If God is in all these forms of things He must also be in the forms of all other things, all things good and beautiful, and all things vile and repulsive, all things lovely and clean, all things filthy and foul. What a very repulsive idea of God is this: a vague vastness, an incomprehensible indefiniteness, filled with an agglomeration of all forms of matter, sheol included.

God must have a personality, an individuality. It is impossible to love, worship, honor and obey a mystic immensity with everything in it. God is omnipresent by virtue of His omniscience. He comprehends, is conscious of everything that transpires anywhere and everywhere through the operation of His own laws and by the exercise of His own will. A being omniscient and omnipotent, infinite in wisdom and in power, is perfectly competent to fix the conditions of his own existence as well as the form of his own personality. The Saviour informs us that God is a spirit.* Whatever His form may be, wherever it

* St. John iv. 24.

is, whatever portion of space it occupies, that is the centre of all space, and from thence emanate all possible degrees and forms of energy.

"XI. In the nature of the finite mind, as such, is to be found the reason why the development of its personal consciousness can take place only through the influences of that cosmic whole which the finite being itself is not, that is, through the stimulation coming from the Non-Ego, not because it needs the contrast with something *alien* in order to have self-existence, but, because, in this respect, as in every other, it does not contain in itself the conditions of its existence. We do not find this limitation in the being of the Infinite; hence, for it alone is there possible a self-existence, which needs neither to be initiated, nor to be continuously developed by something not itself, but which maintains itself within itself with spontaneous action that is eternal and had no beginning.

XII. Perfect personality is in God only; to all finite minds there is allotted but a pale copy thereof. The finiteness of the finite is not a producing condition of this Personality, but a limit and a hindrance of its development."

Such is Lotze's exposition of God's Personality.*

* Microcosmus, vol. II. pp. 687, 688.

XXVIII.

Universes.—Omniverse.—Stellar Systems.—Spheres and Planets.—Life in Them.—Degrees of Light.

OUR new system is composed of seven forms of space, one, the asymptoid, holding in its bowl, as before noted, the six hyperboloids. Each of these latter presents all the features, forces, motions and actions of a universe. Hence we have six universes. As indissolubly united each with all, we may call the grand aggregate system the *Omniverse*, and this omniverse is enveloped by and permeated with the infinite *magnesphere*, whose currents of life and force, infinite in number, are forever coursing towards its vital centre. As each hyperboloid may contain a number of stellar systems, so the asymptoid may contain several celestial systems and spheres that may be transcendental or transfigured forms of the stellar systems within the hyperboloids. By our hypothesis there is but one stellar system in the Asymptoid. In the hyperboloids there may be an indefinite number. The habitable orbs in the former we designate as

Spheres, those in the latter as Planets, and the sentient life existing within these supernal spheres may be more exalted, more spiritual, may approach nearer to the divine, eternal life and spirit. The vital, spiritual succession may be systematic, extending from the centre outward through the asymptoidal and all the hyperboloidal spheres. The life-changes, ascending from the hyperboloidal spheres through those in the asymptoid to the supreme, vital centre, may be similar to the change that the mortal spirit experiences when it passes from earth to paradise. Thus there may be an endless succession of spiritual transformations, each change being from a lower to a loftier and nobler sphere of spiritual life, the constant enlargement of the hyperboloids and the asymptoid providing ample room for every new sphere with the ever-effluent Divinity permeating them all. These spheres may vary in dimensions and increase in number constantly as the asymptoid increases also in its dimensions. We may suppose that a vast number of the planets in the stellar systems are the homes of sentient beings and that *all* the spheres in the asymptoid are likewise so. It is utterly incredible that all these stupendous systems should have been created and set in motion merely to exhibit the power or to gratify a passing fancy of their Creator.

" Life," says Father Secchi, " fills the universe, and with life is associated intelligence; and as beings inferior to ourselves abound, so may there in different conditions exist others of capacity infinitely greater than our own. Between the feeble light of that divine ray which glows in our frail structures, by the help of which also it is permitted us to comprehend so many wonders, and the lofty wisdom of the great Author of all things, there may possibly be interpolated grades of created beings infinite in number, for some of whom theorems which are to us the fruit of arduous studies may be simple intuitions." *

We have remarked the differentiation of the contents of the asymptoid from those of the hyperboloids. We can better appreciate this difference by considering the feebleness of the light of our sun when compared with that of stars of greater magnitude. Sir John Herschel informs us that the intrinsic light of Alpha Centauri, one of the stars nearest to us, is more than twice that of our sun. But the light of Sirius, a star of the first magnitude, is more than four times that of Alpha Centauri; indicating that its intrinsic splendor is sixty-three times that of the sun. As the intrinsic brightness is supposed to afford some indication of their magnitude it follows that Sirius must be immensely larger than our sun. Its light is 26 years

---

* Johnson's Cyc., Art. The Universe, translated from the Italian by the late Pres. Barnard of Columbia College, one of the best polyglot scholars of our time, both in literature and science.

in reaching us. But the light of Capella requires 72 years, about three times as long, and its intrinsic splendor is greater than that of Sirius. Its proportions are bewildering and if our sun were placed between it and Sirius and within photometric range of both, it would cast a shadow upon Sirius, acting as a screen for the light of Capella.

XXIX.

Animal Magnetism ; Psychical and Physical Force ; Spiritualism ; Magnetic Men and Women; Subtle and Extraordinary Magnetic Energy ; Delirium Tremens ; Love ; Devotion ; Saints ; Martyrs ; Procreation of Physical Life ; Heredity ; Pre-natal Impressions ; Seeds and Plants ; Pre-experience ; Reminiscence ; Presentiment ; Dreams.

We have indicated (*supra*) the relation between Spirit and Spiritism. We conceive that the magnetism of the hyperboloids becomes spiritism * in the asymptoid. With the aid of these two forces—spiritism and magnetism—using the former in its diviner sense, we may solve the problem of all life.

The numerous proofs of the existence of animal magnetism presented by Matteucci, Du Bois-Ray-

* It is unfortunate that the use of this term by charlatans and impostors should have made it offensive ; but we ought not to let the abuse of a good thing impair our faith in its value.

mond and others are well known and indisputable. Magnetic fish and birds are equally well known. The correlation between spiritual or psychical, and physical force has been abundantly demonstrated by Charcot, Bernheim, Ribot and other hypnotists and psychologists. The remarkable and undeniable effects produced by so-called spiritualists are due to the same cause.

If we may suppose that magnetism is—next to omnipotence—the fundamental force, the living force, the force that furnishes the *vis-vitæ* of all the natural forces, we may, in the sequel, use this term instead of electricity in the further exposition of our theme.

Dr. Hake sets forth * that " the chemical changes as they occur in the blood system and (are) comprised in the act of oxidation do not result in the evolution of *heat* but *force* which becomes magnetic by the agency of the blood corpuscles ; and this is certainly consistent with what we know of cell life. On this hypothesis, the blood cells form chains and conductors for the magnetic current thus generated, and this is subsequently metamorphosed into heat at every point of the system. On reaching the cerebro-vital centres it becomes vital force "—another name for magnetic force—" and this becomes eventually heat, namely : when it is transmitted to enable the consummation of a vital act, such as sensation, muscular motion or secretion. . . . .

* Kingsett's Animal Chemistry, pp. 180–181.

"The experiments of Du Bois-Raymond in particular go to prove that nerve force is only manifested through media that are not yet met with out of living bodies. On Hake's hypothesis nerve force is derived from the common centre—the brain—where it is stored in the gray matter of which brain matter is partly composed and from which the nerve tubes spread everywhere." He further reasons that " when the cerebro-vital force is united in action within, in the same organic medium with other forces influencing us from without, viz.: light, sound, heat, etc., new results are attained and phenomena of sense and intelligence are observed."

"Electricity is produced," says E. I. Houston,* "during the growth of both animals and plants." During active growth plants form an appreciable source of electricity. Buff has shown that the roots and interior portions of plants are always negatively charged, while the flowers, fruits and green twigs are positively charged.

"Electricity is produced in the bodies of all animals during life. Some animals in addition to this electricity, which is essential to their life, possess the ability to produce sufficiently powerful discharges to serve as a protection against their enemies. This is the case both with the electric eel and the electric ray."

---

* Electricity and Magnetism, p. 67.

All animal tissues, molecules, cells, fibres, nerves, muscles and sinews are good or partial magnetic conductors. Their potential is proportional to the service they are required to perform in order to preserve the normal condition of the organism. When the organism falls into an abnormal condition the change is due to or is followed by a disturbance of the magnetic equilibrium.

We often hear of very magnetic men and women. It is not a mere unmeaning phrase. Very many have met such and acknowledged, without being able to explain, their influence. It is by one form of this force—magnetic—that the orator, the poet, the story-teller, hold and charm their audiences. It is this force that produces panics in excited crowds. It is by this force that the body, when the brain is in an abnormal condition, through delirium tremens or an epileptic fit, is charged with five-fold its normal strength, so that five men can hardly restrain one man. And yet, there is no change in the mechanism. It is the stimulus that is applied to the brain that produces this vast increase of power. This is also especially notable in men who are enraged or crazed. They perform wonderful feats of strength when excited of which they are utterly incapable in their sober moments.

The extraordinary deeds of valor recorded as having been performed by the leaders and knights of the crusades and by heroes and their followers in every earnestly-contested defensive or aggresive war are not exaggerated. They are only reports of simple facts. It is this force that enables men to endure the severest hardships and trials, to defy, if not to conquer, fate.

It is this force that awakens love at first sight. It is the vibration of this force through the eyes that thrills the hearts of the lover and the loved. It is this force that inspires the soldier's courage, the mother's love, the saint's devotion, the martyr's constancy and the bigot's zeal. By this force prayer is borne heavenward. It swells the anthem of praise, the song of joy, the shout of gladness, the carol of birds, and develops the weird notes of the singing flame.

But the intensest manifestation of this force is the procreation of physical life. It is only necessary to suggest the immense intensity of the sexual passion, the delirium of love. Remove, eliminate entirely that sentiment and its concomitants, that irresistible magnetic attraction, from the physical constitution, and all animal life would soon cease from the earth.

Mark the horse as portrayed by Job: "The glory of his nostrils is terrible. He paweth in the valley, and rejoiceth in his strength. He mocketh at fear, and is not affrighted; he swalloweth the ground with fierceness and rage, and he smelleth the battle afar off." Observe the stallion when, in the season, he is led forth for exercise. Mark his expanded nostrils, his flashing eyes, his mobile ears, his magnificent crest, his silken, shining coat, his distended veins and muscles, his lofty, elastic tread which seems scarcely to touch the earth, and his vigorous and graceful motions. What an embodiment of passion and of power, and what a magnificent magneto-calorific machine!

The perpetuation of the human race involves the awful responsibilities of heredity. We know the inexorable fidelity with which parental traits, both physical and mental, are transmitted to the offspring. It is one of the most remarkable instances of the persistence of force. And one of the most extraordinary phenomena of heredity is the one by which any particular trait may be emphasized by a pre-natal impression or influence, commonly known as the "birth-mark."

In these cases a sudden and strong excitement of the brain and nerve-power of the mother causes great surprise or fear, such as seeing some very repulsive object or some scene in which certain objects, attractive or repulsive, are specially noticeable. The result is that an indelible mark or image is fixed upon the body of the unborn infant. This is an instance in which the psychical and physical forces act at once and together in perfect accord.

"Sensations and ideas," says Lewes, "spring up in the mind as flowers spring up in the field. . . . . Science is prompted to seek out the conditions of their appearance, their changes and their disappearance. .... We know that a seed placed in suitable soil will throw out root and stem. We can trace its development as it draws certain materials from the soil and the atmosphere. But we know (also) that the seed itself is a product, and has its own special determinism. The forms which the seed assumes are partly peculiar to it and partly common to myriads of others, nay, some of its forms are common to all plants whatever."

Concerning the electricity of plants, the following conclusions were arrived at by Wartman (Bibliothèque Universelle de Genève, Dec, 1850), after an investigation continued for two years:—

"1. Electric currents are to be detected in all parts of vegetables but those furnished with insulating substances, old bark, etc., etc.

"2. These currents occur at all times and seasons, and even when the portion examined is separated from the body of the plant, as long as it continues moist.

"3. In the roots, stems, branches, petioles, and peduncles, there exists a central descending and a peripherical ascending current; Wartman calls them axial currents.

"4. Lateral currents may be detected passing from the layers of the stem where the liber and alburnum touch, to the surrounding parts.

"5. In the leaf the current passes from the lamina to the nerves as well as to the central parts of the petiole and stalk.

" 6. In the flowers the currents are feeble. They are very marked in the succulent fruits, and in some kinds of grain; the currents from fruits proceeding in most cases from the superficial parts to the adjacent organs. The strength of the currents depends on the season, they are greatest in the spring when the plant is bathed in sap.

" 7. Currents can also be detected proceeding from the plant to the soil, which is thus positive with relation to it, and currents are also manifested when two distinct plants are placed in the circuit of the rheometer."

These results were confirmed by Becquerel (Comptes-Rendus, Nov. 4, 1850). He ascertained particularly the determination of electrical currents from the pith of the wood to the bark, which shows that the earth in the act of vegetation continually acquires an excess of positive electricity; and the parenchyma of the bark and a part of the wood an excess of negative electricity, which is transmitted to the air by means of the vapor of exhaled water; and the opposite electrical states of vegetables and the earth give reason to think that, from the enormous vegetation in some parts of the globe, they must exert some influence on the electric phenomena of the atmosphere.

Flashes of light have been seen to be emitted from many flowers, principally orange-colored flowers, soon after sunset on sultry days; this phenomenon was diligently studied by Zawadski;

he noticed that it occurred most frequently in the months of July and August, and he observed that the same flower discharged a number of flashes in succession.*

From the bosom of the earth have been gathered, since the first appearance of man upon it, all the grains and other forms of vegetable nourishment that help to sustain his body and promote its physical growth. The germs of the last year's growth of these numerous and varied forms of life were contained in the seeds of their generators of the preceding year, and thus it hath been, and thus it will continue to be in all the coming years. Whence cometh this vitality? And how is the peculiar and individual form of vitality secured to each of the myriad germs? What was the origin of what has been happily designated as the "*determinism*" of these germs, the function which gave them their peculiar character? That determinism is as much a creation of, or derivation from, the Omnipotent Power as is the soul or spiritual faculty of man. Is it the will of the plant? Why should the infinitesimal germ perpetuate one form of life more than another, and this invariably, and with unfailing certainty through all ages? Simply because that determinism is a manifestation of the *Will* of God through fixed laws.

Says St. Paul,† "And that which thou sowest,

* Noad Text Book of Electricity, p. 13, 14, 15.
† I. Corinthians, xv. 37, 38.

thou sowest not that body that shall be, but bare grain, it may chance of wheat, or of some other grain : But God giveth it a body as it hath pleased Him, and to every seed its own body."

"There are," says Lewes, "conditions and pre-conditions of experience as there are conditions and pre-conditions of plant life." Many persons who have experienced bodily suffering from wounds or from the loss of limbs have described, and insisted that they feel a return, a distinct reminder of their suffering on each anniversary of its occurrence. An African traveller (Dr. Livingstone?), was wounded by a lion in the interior of Africa. Annually on the return of the day on which he was wounded the pain of the wound was renewed.

Many soldiers who have lost limbs in battle have insisted that on the return of the day when they were amputated they *felt* their presence with little or no suffering. Has the old Pythagorean doctrine of pre-existence a realistic foundation?

Are we subject to some persistent, subtle force that has a wave-length of twelve months' duration? Are these indications or suggestions of those twilight reminiscences of events and scenes of the long-ago and far-away that come back to us with a force and vividness that almost compel us to believe that they are the return, the resurrection of long-forgotten realities, while at the same time we are certain that they have never formed any part of our mortal experience? Are they wave-motions of a past existence which are to roll on through the endless hereafter? Are they connecting links between the mortal and immortal spirit, the sentiency that has lived through all the past and will live on through all the future?

These re-cognitions are beyond the reach of *experiment*, but there are few thoughtful persons with whom they have not been incidents of *experience*. The faculties of reminiscence and presentiment are among the most subtle and interesting phenomena of psychology. We can cultivate and strengthen the memory, and thereby increase our store of knowledge; but no possible training can enable us to recall the vast number of scenes and events which have constituted the whole experience of our past lives. Yet the enduring and ever-sentient mental palimpsest may restore them to our cognizance when it is liberated from the fleshly tabernacle.

" Inasmuch as the idea of a movement is only an idea of a sensory impression," says Ferrier (Functions of the Brain, p. 389), " visual, tactile and others, which coincide with the particular movement, it seems quite possible that persons who have had a limb amputated may be able to picture a movement of the limb, just as a blind man may recall a scene when he can no longer see," then he quotes cases mentioned by Weir-Mitchell, of persons who have had an arm amputated and are able to write and apparently execute a movement of the hand, and also to feel the pain of the amputation, the stronger the will the stronger the pain. But these are very different from the cases above referred to. These last are wholly involuntary sensations impressed upon the mind or recalled to the memory entirely independent of the will, and accompanied by a sense of pain that the will cannot inflict. We have a more or less acute sense of pain in our dreams, and so have the victims of catalepsy or delirium tremens ; but it is wholly involuntary.

We know the marvellous activity, at times, of the brain when the body is asleep. We dream of exercising the five senses, of doing everything we are capable of doing when awake. And we dream of doing work in a few moments, of finishing tasks, of performing feats, mental and physical, that would require days to accomplish during our waking hours.

If the spirit is so wonderfully active when connected with the body, how intense must be that activity when it is disembodied, when it has shuffled off this mortal coil. Its intensified consciousness and power of perception must enable it to comprehend, as it were, instantaneously a succession of acts and events which could only be the result of a comparatively long mortal experience occupying a considerable lapse of time. And this power of comprehension, this quickness of perception are to continue forever, constantly acquiring knowledge, constantly accumulating wisdom, constantly approaching Deity. And this must be the supreme bliss of immortality, the perpetual inspiration of the "everlasting song."

·If the comprehension of the mortal spirit can be so intensely active, how intense, instantaneous, imminent and effective must be the comprehension, the ever-consciousness, of God!

Dreams differ from presentiments in that they may present to the mind images and incidents both of the past and the future. In both dreams and presentiments the images, scenes and incidents presented to the mind may be agreeable, joyous, delightful, or disagreeable, painful, torturing. In some cases the suffering is intense. It is doubtful whether the martyr at the stake suffers more agony bodily than does the victim of delirium tremens mentally.

But far more subtle and occult is the faculty, if such it may be called, of presentiment. It is entirely beyond the possibility of *pre*-experience. It is a *pre*sentment of something that lies in the future and is to be presented, made known to us. It is the psychologic analogue of inspiration, prophecy.

Some years ago a writer in the Atlantic Monthly Magazine expressed himself as "curious to know whether the recurrence of the same dream or the same class of dreams for long periods is a common experience." I doubt not that it is a somewhat frequent, if not common, experience, and at that time I recorded, but did not publish, the following experience of my own:

For nearly half a century, at intervals varying from six to twenty-four months and growing a little longer with the lapse of years, one remarkable dream has been impressed upon my mind with unusual force and distinctness. It is this: that I was endowed with an inherent force that enabled me to overcome the action of gravity and move through space in any direction but always in curves with a wave-like motion and with different velocities. There was a constant, conscious and vigorous exercise of the will in controlling and directing the motor-power, which seemed to have its origin in the brain and chest, and was as distinctly felt as what is called a thrill, differing from this only that it was continuous. The bodily investiture was a flowing robe of ample dimensions and graceful form. The arms were generally folded on the breast but the right arm sometimes waved in gestures to friends beneath. No particular use was made of the nether limbs except to pose them gracefully as the variation of the movements might require. During a number of the earliest of these visitations the predominant feeling was one of wonder and surprise that the subject of them had acquired such a novel and mysterious means of locomotion and with much pleasurable excitement he called attention to it. There seemed to be no particular end in view, no special purpose to be accomplished. It was a condition of active, carefree enjoyment. It was not like flying, for the mechanism of wings was entirely wanting. The motion was produced and governed by an inherent energy, a latent, odyllic force that was perfectly controlled by the will. The sensation excited was like that which we may suppose is experienced by soaring birds as they traverse the air.

For some years these visitations occurred within the walls of a room and in the presence of friends, the former growing larger in size and the latter increasing in number. But after a time there were changes. The first was this: The dreamer was with a large party of friends who had gone out in a beautiful June day to absorb the electric sunlight, to breathe the bracing ozonic air and to recreate with the birds, the flowers and the trees. The strange power became operative. The dreamer rose in the air and circled round in wide and wider curves—calm, serene, buoyant and happy in the exercise of this strange power; regarding his friends who were looking up to him from below, with infinite interest and wishing that they might be similarly endowed and join him in his aerial flights. High and higher he soared, and fast and faster he swept around the widening horizons, returning again and again to his friends with increasing satisfaction and regard. The serene and pleasurable emotions with which he began his flights were soon changed to exuberant gladness, exultant joy and profound gratitude for this marvellous gift. As is often the case in dreams, the matter was logically discussed with friends and it was settled that this was not a mere dream but a marvellous reality by which a mortal had been miraculously endowed. The vision at each return may have occupied ten minutes' time, but the dreamer seemed to have enjoyed some hours of great happiness.

After having these remarkable visions at various intervals for more than forty years, the intervals growing longer with increasing age, another change occurred, the mode of motion changed. Instead of soaring upward the dreamer sat on a handsome hand-sled such as he used in his boyhood. Seated on this with his feet on the front bar he seemed to be endowed with the same marvellous power with which he rose into the air and by the aid of which he propelled the sled with great velocity across ice or well-beaten snow-paths. There were no friends or spectators to witness these rides, and a singular circumstance was they did not terminate at any particular place, but both the dreamer and the sled seemed to vanish in the air.

Now a word as to the origin of these visions. When a boy of twelve years, more than threescore and ten years ago, I went "to meeting" as all New England people did in those days, in the old-fashioned "meeting-house" with its two galleries with a high, arched ceiling between them and a row of windows opening into each. On a beautiful June Sunday, the windows being open, two swallows flew into one of them. Rising into the arch overhead they circled around chirruping and coqueting with each other in the most charming manner and attracting the attention of the whole congregation. As I watched them from the "boys' seat" in the "men's gallery" I became more interested in them than in the sermon and, boy-like, my imagination took flight with the swallows. I thought what a charming way it was to move about; what delightful sensations they must experience as they swept around in their wave-like undulations with no ruts or stones or other obstacles to impede their exhilarating flight which they could arrest and renew at will.

Then I thought of our Sunday-school teachings concerning the angels who, bearing messages of love or performing deeds of mercy, swept on exulting wings through boundless space, companions of, stars and travellers of the Milky Way. This was the root-conception of the soaring dream. That of the terrestrial gliding had a different origin. In those days there were no fancy sleds for sale and the boys were dependent on home-production. My brother and myself had a famous one, a regular frame sled made by a wagonmaker and shod with thin strap-iron runners ground smooth. The velocity with which it rushed down the steep New England hills literally took our breath away so that we were obliged to turn our heads sidewise in order to breathe. The speed acquired was such as to take us a comparatively long way across the levels at the foot of the hills. We had no successful rivals and the exercise was most exhilarating. The mental impression was carried into future years and developed in our dream. The first of the dreams did not transpire until more than a score of years after the events described.

XXX.

Thought-transference; Mind Reading; Spiritualism; Personal Experience; Systematic Investigation; Amazing Developments; Aerial Music; Music from Piano Keys, with Harp Accompaniment on the Strings; Piano beating time to its own tune; Trance Speaking and Writing; Planchette; Mental Conversation.

AMONG "influences" to be investigated Bacon * mentions "the sympathy of distant objects, the transmission of impressions from spirit to spirit no less than from body to body." The psychologic phenomena of mind-reading and thought-transference, and also the remarkable exhibitions of the spiritualists, are so well known that it is not necessary to quote the evidence of Owen, Charcot, Ribot, Bernheim, Bjonstrom and other writers to confirm them.

As something original in this direction we shall relate some within our own experience, and, in so doing, speak in the first person singular in the closing sentences.

* Nov. Org., Aph. 31.

Judge S., a distinguished jurist, Mr. P., a distinguished graduate of Cambridge, who finished his classical education at Heidelburg and Breslau, with myself and nine others, undertook, in a quiet way, and purely in the interest of science, to investigate the phenomena of spiritualism. Of this circle of twelve, six were ladies and six gentlemen, all educated Christian people who met fortnightly in their own homes. There were two impressionists who possessed spiritual gifts, one a young woman, twenty-seven years of age, of respectable Methodist parentage, with limited education, modest in demeanor and in delicate health. The other was a respectable and successful country merchant in the prime of life and in perfect health.

Neither ever exhibited in public or for gain. The young woman developed into a writing medium, with the additional power imparted by a certain prescience of the mysterious force that enabled her to interpret it verbally without going into the trance state.

The gentleman was a subjective medium, that is, the force took possession of him and governed his actions. Most of the phenomena were exhibited in half-lights, but occasionally in daylight. We could always see the action of the mediums. When we met, the ladies and gentlemen, by directions received through Miss B., sat alternately in a circle. Half of them were members of church choirs, with fair musical accomplishments. The first spiritual requirement was the singing of a certain metrical version of the Lord's Prayer, which was duly rendered by the singers, and in the last line there was generally a sweet, plaintive accompaniment from a voice in the air.

Then followed the phenomenal performances. A heavy square-box piano was placed in one corner of the room with the key-board close to the wall and the top raised full height. At the free corner of the piano sat Miss B., with her right hand on it. Various musical numbers were performed by the keys alone. The most remarkable one was called "The Wreck," which set forth musically the wreck of a ship in a terrible gale. The performance was amazing in its grandeur and sublimity. Commencing with a cheerful, moderately animated strain, like a ship leaving harbor before a pleasant breeze, with the water gently plashing its prow, it gradually became stronger and louder until the wind grew to a gale and the gale to a hurricane. The roaring of the wind, the whistling noise among the shrouds, the tearing and flapping of the sails, the hissing of the waves, the great breaking swash of the water over the decks, the creaking of the timbers, the groaning and breaking of the masts, and the snapping of the cordage as they went by the board, and finally the muffled, gurgling sound with which she went down, was given with a fearful vividness and power that literally made our hair stand on end. We could feel the strong undulations of the mighty force of sound as it vibrated along the floor and trembled in our chairs. At times it seemed as though every string in the instrument must be broken and its frame burst asunder.

At other times we were favored with exquisite renderings of familiar airs. Occasionally with these there was exhibited this remarkable phenomenon: while the keys were giving the air, a delightful harp-accompaniment was performed on the strings of the instrument in a note above or below the air itself. The effect was weird and delightful in the extreme.

Sometimes a waltz would be followed by a rattling fugue in which all the strings seemed to be taxed beyond their utmost strength, as though all the bolts of Jove were thundering through them. During all this time the medium was sitting with one hand on the corner of the piano, but not near enough to the keys to reach them even if she had desired to do so.

The furniture and other articles were set in motion, until the room was alive with their antics. Sofa-cushions, chairs, books and papers waltzed and galloped with each other in the most ludicrous manner. A flute lying on a table was taken apart and its joints sent to take part in this devil's dance. A bell on the mantle was lifted and jingled vigorously.

But the most amazing exhibition of force was presented by the heavy piano while a lively tune was played by the keys. It was lifted bodily from the floor, and then the *time* of the air was gently beaten on the floor by one of the legs, all the rest of the instrument being in the air. Let it be borne in mind that there was sufficient light in the room to permit us to see all these actions.

On another occasion the performances were suddenly checked and the hostess of that evening— Mrs. Dr. S.—was directed to send away "those persons that were listening in the adjoining room" —the front parlor. Entering it with a light the two servant girls were found without their shoes, listening at the partition wall. Of course we knew nothing of their presence.

With the male medium we had the following experiences : He was directed, through Miss B., to stand in the centre of the room, and two ladies and two gentlemen were directed to inclose him within their joined hands. He then was thrown into a trance. His right hand was raised straight above his head. He asked that a lead-pencil should be put in it, which was done. Then his hand began to move as if in the act of writing. When its motion ceased it fell by his side and we were directed, through Miss B., to search the walls. The ceiling of the room was high and arched. The ground color of the paper covering the side walls was a pale lemon, the figures being vines and leaves in neutral tints.

On one corner of the white ceiling, just above the cornice, we found written in excellent chirography—the text-letters being more than half an inch long and the capitals in proportion—these words, "God is Love." In the other corner of the same side was written in the same style, "God is Light." On one of the end walls was the single word "Harmony," written diagonally upward on the ground color of the paper. The medium stated that he felt the tremor or vibration imparted to his fingers through the pencil as in the act of writing but had no idea what he wrote.

He was then directed to take his stand in front of the mantelpiece and, passing into a trance, he began the delivery of a most animating harangue in a pleasant, liquid Indian dialect, conspicuous for the absence of labials and the accentuation of all the vowels. We were within four miles of the Tuscarora Reservation in Niagara County. He was frequently interrupted by the most hearty applause, given apparently, by a band of Indians gathered near him on his right front. This applause was given *viva-voce* in Indian dialect and by clapping hands. Judging from its vigor and the number of voices, it seemed that there must have been a hundred or more in the audience.

The medium, retaining his position and trance condition, followed this performance with a most eloquent speech in Hungarian, the spell of Kossuth's eloquence still lingering in the country after his then recent departure. It was received with grave and earnest applause by a gathering of invisible Magyars who seemed to be as numerous as the Indians. When the medium came out of his trance he nearly lost his balance, and was assisted by one of the gentlemen present.

Prof. Crooke in the article on Spiritualism published many years since in the "British Quarterly Review," which created such a sensation at the time, mentions the case of a medium who experienced, although in perfect health, a remarkable change in weight. A curious effect of this force on our male medium was that in two years his *head* was enlarged so that he was obliged to wear a hat a size larger than he had been accustomed to wear. This was a growth similar to some magnetic growths, so to call them, described in the sequel.

Another experience, of which I will write in the first person singular, was the following: Being in the city of Brooklyn, N. Y., I made a morning call on a young married lady, a relative, an educated, accomplished woman, a fine musician, of genial and magnetic temperament. The evening before at a social gathering, she had been much interested in the performance of a Planchette there exhibited when that mysterious piece of mechanism was first introduced in this country.

As I had not seen one, she borrowed of her friend the one they had used. It responded to her touch but not to mine. She had been a church member for a number of years, and would have been shocked at the slightest suggestion of any contact with spiritualism. But my previous experience enabled me to divine at once the character of the developments. She asked several questions, to which correct answers, as she stated, were written on the blank paper on which it stood. She then asked, "who is this gentleman with me?" My name was correctly written in reply. Then I asked, "is any one present willing to communicate with me." "Yes," was the written answer. "Who is it?" After a pause the reply was "Edith," the name of a beautiful and precocious child of twelve summers who had died eight years before of a disease, the precise character of which the doctors could not determine.

After several other questions, to which accurate answers were given, I asked, "Edith, can you answer *mental* questions?" The written reply was, "Yes." I then asked her mentally many questions about persons whom she had known, about scenes with which she had been familiar, about different events and changes that had occurred since her death. In reply to the question as to what caused her death, the answer was "peritonitis," a word she never could have heard during her life and the import of which she did not know. The promptness and correctness of her answers concerning various events and changes, births, deaths, marriages, social and neighborhood incidents, were startling. After many tests of this character I asked mentally, " Edith, does my mind react upon itself through the agency of this instrument, or does your mind respond to mine!" The answer was: " My mind responds directly to yours through it." Finally, my parting thought was this: " Well, dear Edith, I expect to leave for home to-morrow; have you any message for mother or sister L.?" Reply, "Only dear love and tell them to be prepared to meet me here."

It will be noted that these questions were all mentally suggested without the utterance of a sound, and that my lady friend had only two fingers of one hand on the instrument, and all the answers were written promptly, connectedly and distinctly. At no time while the interview was progressing did I touch the instrument.

After these experiences it is impossible for me to doubt that, under favorable conditions, there may be communion between the spirits of those who are mortal and of those who have put on immortality.

The persistence of natural forces and the indestructibility of matter are demonstrated, undoubted truths. It is entirely unphilosophical, unreasonable and illogical to suppose that spirit which dominates matter, makes it subservient to its convenience, its use and its pleasure, is not more emphatically absolute, persistent and indestructible. Since the experiences here recorded I have never found it convenient or practicable to pursue the subject further.

We cannot resist the temptation to record here another remarkable instance of spiritual influence upon the mind furnished by Miss Elizabeth Doten at the close of a lecture delivered in Boston some years ago. Miss Doten was, at that time, a young woman of respectable parentage, irreproachable character and uneducated. She was entirely incompetent to originate or parody any respectable poetical composition in her normal state. She could, no more than many others, give any satisfactory explanation of her peculiar gift. The piece is a remarkable parody of Poe's most remarkable poem, The Raven.

I.

From the throne of life eternal,
From the home of love supernal
Where the angel feet make music over all the stony floor—
Mortals, I have come to meet you,
Come with words of peace to greet you
And to tell you of the glory that is mine forevermore.

II.

Once before I found a mortal
Waiting at the heavenly portal—
Waiting but to catch some echo from that ever-opening door:
Then I seized his quickened being,
And, through all his inward seeing,
Caused my burning inspiration in a fiery flood to pour!

III.

Now I come more meekly human,
And the poor weak lips of woman
Touch with fire from off the altar, not with burnings as of
yore,
But in holy love descending,
With her chastened being blending,
I would fill your souls with music from the bright celestial
shore.

IV.

As one heart yearns for another,
As a child turns to his mother,
From the golden gates of glory turn I to the earth once more,
Where I drained the cup of sadness,
Where my soul was stung to madness,
And life's bitter, burning billows, swept my burdened being
o'er.

V.

Here the harpies and the ravens,
Human vampyres—sordid cravens—
Preyed upon my soul and substance till I writhed in anguish
sore;
Life and I seemed mismated,
For I felt accursed and fated,
Like a restless, wrathful spirit, wandering on the Stygian
shore.

VI.

Tortured by a nameless yearning,
Like a frost-fire, freezing, burning,
Did the purple pulsing life-tide through its fevered channels
pour,
'Till the golden bowl—life's token—
Into shining shards was broken,
And my chained and chafing spirit leapt from out its prison
door.

VII.

But while living, striving, dying,
Never did my soul cease crying :
"Ye who guide the fates and furies, give, oh! give me, I implore,
From the myriad hosts of nations,
From the countless constellations,
One pure spirit that can love me—one that I, too, can adore!"

VIII.

Through this fervent aspiration
Found my fainting soul salvation,
For from out its blackened fire-crypts did my quickened spirit soar ;
And my beautiful ideal—
Not too saintly to be real—
Burst more brightly on my vision than the fancy-formed Lenore.

IX.

'Mid the surging seas she found me,
With the billows breaking round me,
And my saddened, sinking spirit, in her arms of love implore;
Like a lone one, weak and weary,
Wandering in the midnight dreary,
On her sinless, saintly bosom, brought me to the heavenly shore.

X.

Like the breath of blossoms blending,
Like the prayers of saints ascending,
Like the rainbow's seven-hued glory, blend our souls forevermore.
Earthly love and lust enslaved me,
But divinest love hath saved me,
And I know now, first and only, how to love and to adore.

XI.

Oh, my mortal friends and brothers,
We are each and all another's,
And the soul that gives most freely from its treasure hath the more.
Would you lose your life, you find it;
And in giving love you bind it,
Like an amulet of safety, to your heart forevermore!

The rhythm and alliteration are as marvellous as in the original. No genius could have written this and then allowed Miss Doten to commit it to memory and claim it as an inspiration of her own, spiritual or otherwise.

There are no facts or truths connected with human history that are more thoroughly authenticated and established than those regarding the intimate connection and communion of the Infinite and the finite mind. The Old and New Testaments contain abundant records of their inter-communions. The Prophets and Apostles were its most illustrious mediums, the Saviour being the immediate and absolute representative of Deity. It is not creditable to the status of occidental Psychology and Biology that it declines or neglects to systematically and thoroughly investigate the spiritual and the cognate forces. This investigation in all its branches cannot well be pursued by single individuals. We know that there are certain magnetic currents that increase their potency when they work together side by side. So with spiritual and occult forces. They are most potent when a number of them are united in action. But it is the spirit that actuates the investigators, the motive that prompts their labor that is of most vital consequence. When a chemist resolves to study some new substance said to possess valuable properties that may be useful, sanitarily or otherwise, he does not begin in a doubting skeptical temper, prejudging it perhaps as a bit of quackery that he will expose; on the contrary, he makes due preparation and determines to study the case in a kindly, earnest, receptive spirit, and it is only in this spirit that such subjects can be successfully investigated.

XXXI.

Remarkable Action of a Subtle Force, Reappearance of Lost Articles.

I MAY here record a few instances of the remarkable action of a subtle force, that, if not magnetism, must have been spiritual. The first notice of the action of a similar force is recorded in the last verses of the eighth chapter of Acts, when Philip after baptizing the Ethiopian was "caught away" and "was found at Azotus." It is necessary to give some particulars in order that the phenomena may be understood.

In 1877 my residence was, as it had been nearly forty years, at Niagara Falls, N. Y. My house and grounds, garden included, were on the shore of the great river just above the American rapids. The outlook from my bedroom was eastward across the garden and up the river. Next the window, north, stood a bureau, then a closet, with washstand in opposite corner. A chair, always used in disrobing and dressing, stood in front of the bureau. On retiring one night in the latter part of June, 1877, I missed my gold eyeglasses. The next morning I found them in a favorite strawberry bed over which I had been working the previous afternoon. Two weeks later I missed them again and not finding them I bought a new pair in a cellulose frame. In the morning when dressing I always sat in the chair in front of the bureau near the bed.

Six months after losing the glasses, one morning, on rising, I occupied the chair as usual, and after getting on my nether garments and performing the usual ablution at the washstand, I returned to the bureau, and using the mirror standing on it put on my neck-tie. On turning to get my vest which, with the coat, hung on the chair-back, I saw the gold glasses lying on the bottom of the chair which I had occupied but a few minutes before. It was a surprise, for it was winter, and the coat and vest were not the same I had worn when the glasses were lost. I could not solve the mystery, and the circumstance passed out of my mind. About a year afterward I lost the gold glasses again and resumed the use of the cellulose pair which I had laid aside after finding the gold ones which I never saw again. Within two months I lost the cellulose glasses, and then had double half-lenses for reading and far-seeing put in my gold spectacles.

In 1881, after a sore domestic bereavement left me alone in my house, I removed to Ithaca to make my home with the last survivor of my children, the wife of Prof. I. P. Church.

In the autumn of the year 1882, I went to Niagara on business, and took a chamber in my house then occupied by a tenant. My baggage consisted of a double valise of moderate size with a swinging partition between the two compartments. Its interior was lined with cloth, without folds or creases. Its contents were a dress-suit, shirts, collars, cuffs, handkerchiefs, socks, and other small articles. On taking possession of my room I put the dress-suit, coat, vest and pantaloons and the shirts in the drawers of a bureau standing in a corner opposite the bed, and on the top of the bureau I put some toilet articles, leaving nothing in the valise but some handkerchiefs and socks. The dress-suit I had worn repeatedly, always emptying the pockets after use.

When ready to pack my valise to return to Ithaca, I took it up, opened it, turned it bottom up, emptying the few contents on the bed, and then placed it, right side up, in a chair at the foot of the bed. I then went to the bureau, took from the drawer the dress-suit—which I had had no occasion to wear—and on returning to the valise to put it in I saw lying in the middle of one of the compartments the lost eyeglasses which I had not seen for nearly a year. By what mysterious agency they came out of the unknown and into the valise I cannot divine.

These two instances of the exhibition of this peculiar force were surprising, but the next one I have to relate was bewildering. Like the others it needs a word of preface. I carried when traveling, a small tortoise-shell comb in a morocco case. The comb was of peculiar shape the back being straight, the teeth at one end about five-eighths of an inch long, and at the other end a little shorter. On one occasion while using it to comb out a wire-tooth hair-brush, one of the teeth near the broad end was broken out. I carried it in a vest-pocket and only when traveling. In May, 1893, expecting to spend some weeks at the World's Fair, I had made by a city tailor a suit, coat, vest, and pantaloons for the summer's wear. When they were sent home I put them on and found that the pantaloons needed some alteration. This was made by the tailor and they were returned. On taking them to my room, opening the package and shaking out the garment *that comb without the case* dropped on the carpet. I was indeed astonished, for I had not seen it for ten years, and then it was in the case and in a bureau drawer. That it was the same comb was demonstrated by its peculiar shape and the lost tooth. At the tailor's where the garment was made nothing of the kind had been seen. Such are the simple facts in these three cases of the re-appearance of lost articles.

XXXII.

Personal Experience in Animal Magnetism; Results; Physical and Mental.

As connected with the subject of personal animal magnetism, I may be pardoned for saying, that in my younger days and during the prime of life, I had the power to exhibit that force in certain directions in a remarkable manner, both voluntarily and involuntarily. Involuntarily, while reading sublime or unusually impressive passages from Isaiah, Shakespeare, Dante, Goethe or other authors of similar intellectual power. At such times I felt a thrill commencing at the brain and coursing through the nervous system precisely similar to the excitement produced by holding in the hands, or applying to any part of the body, the electrodes of an electric machine. The only difference was that the vibrations through the nerves were more rapid than those through the conductors, so that the sensation was like the steady flow of a uniform current. At the same time I could feel the effect in the roots of the hair on my head, though the force was not sufficient to raise it on end.

It was sufficient, however, to elevate the short, fine hirsute filaments growing more sparsely on other parts of the body. This was especially true of those growing on the lower limbs, particularly on the front side from the knee upward, and I cultivated this faculty to such an extent that by putting the foot of the bare leg on a chair I could repeat striking passages from any favorite author and see and feel the filaments as they rose and fell with the varying sensations.

This is simply the function exercised by the dog and the cat, especially when excited, and it is conclusive proof that hair is a good magnetic conductor. The experiment of Laër noted on page 44 is confirmatory of the same fact. On page 31 we have shown that pointed magnets are more effective than spheres, cylinders or any solid with blunt ends, and that the greatest magnetic power is developed at the points. This is as true of hair as of any other conductor.

NOTE.—It may serve a practical purpose to note here that the quality, the fineness and beauty of human hair are injured by cutting. When examined under the microscope human hair, as well as all other in its natural condition, is found to be pointed at the end. After it is cut, at whatever age, the end presents a flat surface. Thenceforward its tendency is to grow more rapidly and coarser and it never again becomes sharp pointed. To secure the maximum fineness, beauty and gloss, the hair should never be cut. If allowed to grow uncut it will attain and never exceed a certain length and will be as fine and glossy as it possibly can be. A young kinsman whose mother secured him immunity from shears was saved thereby much time, temper, trouble and expense during his life. The hirsute appendages of his head and face were fine, soft and shining and never exceeded a certain length. These facts suggest that the hair of females never should be cut except for sanitary reasons.

Neither should men be shaven and shorn, except for the same reasons or as a matter of convenience. Both women and men might be excused from coveting the lustre of the Indian's sable locks. Individuals whose hair when shortened exhibits the "cow-lick" so-called, may avoid it by permitting the hair to grow to a reasonable length. It would seem that the ludicrousness of its appearance, especially on adults, would prompt its prevention by any reasonable means.

I could also, when startled by an unusual sound, feel a motion in the left ear. This sensitiveness I likewise cultivated, and could, at any time, by the exercise of the will, so move the ear as to make its motion visible to others. This I could not do with the right-side ear.

The sense of vision was also unusually strong. I could recognize objects at a greater distance than could other persons of equal health and strength. To this strong visual power was due the fact that I could retain, for an unusual period—three to five minutes—the ocular spectrum left in the eyes when they are closed, after looking steadily for a moment at a distinctly colored object. This spectrum is, at first view, invariably of the same color as the object seen, but gradually assumes its complementary color. This spectral image is always erect and much larger than any image revealed by the opthalmoscope.

The *thrills* noted above were often experienced, and generally with marked, sometimes with intense, effect. The grand view from a mountain top; the purple tops of the mountains themselves as seen against the azure sky; the ocean, tempest-tossed, and its mighty waves breaking upon the cliffs and hissing around the huge boulders of a rock-bound shore; an angry storm with the roaring wind swaying, breaking and uprooting the forest trees; or a heavy thunder-storm with the lightning's sharp flash and crash and the rolling thunder's huge waves of sound dying away in the distance; the first view of peerless Niagara on a peerless autumn day, with its iris-bar'd arms lifted heavenward and bathed in sunshine, while its solemn monotone sounded a perpetual anthem to its Creator's praise; scenes like these excited the utmost tension of the nerves and every hirsute filament stood erect like a tiny wire, which it was painful forcibly to repress.

In contrast with these, the contemplation of the stars which seem both to send to the spirit messages of love and to beckon it upward, especially the study of that star-paved galaxy that spans the sunless dome; the calm and gently pulsing ocean laving and dallying with the silver sand upon its sunny beach and tossing back to the sun his brilliant rays; a gorgeous sunset; the fully arched covenant bow; the peaceful valley with its winding stream bordered with wild flowers, vocal with the hum of bees, and smiling in the light and warmth of a June-lit day; the blossom and the breath of flowers; the song of birds; a beautiful painting or any surpassingly beautiful work of art; the autumn woods transfigured and glorified with color; an exquisite bit of sculptured marble that almost speaks and breathes; and more especially the perfect face and form of a beautiful woman beautifully adorned; all these thrilled the heart with gladness and filled the eyes with tears. However weak or otherwise it may be, I have to confess that every "thing of beauty," the expression of every inspiring thought, every sublime aspiration, every noble sentiment commands the homage, the sacrifice of tears.

Thunder-storms possessed a peculiar fascination for me in my boyhood. It was a pervasive satisfaction and pleasure after the first heavy rainfall was over, particularly in the evening, to go out and climb a tree or the highest fence to watch the electric explosions and listen to the reverberating thunder. There was a leap of ecstasy at each discharge and in watching the electric ribbon that marked its eccentric course from the zenith to the horizon.

Another evening fascination was to lie on a flat rock near a huge oak tree, on the hillside shore of a beautiful lake, and gaze up at the stars.

"A boy's will is the wind's will, and a boy's thoughts are long, long thoughts." It was an unwearying delight to look up at the calm, patient, persistent, inscrutable stars, to dream dreams concerning them, and to wonder what they were and what was the lesson they could teach.

A notable phenomenon that attended the copious thunder-showers of the spring and early summer was the invigorating effect of breathing the purified air after they were over, air that was laden with ozone and charged with sulphur. The odor of the latter was very decided, and frequently its presence was manifested by the appearance of a pale yellow film on the surface of the rain-water gathered in the depressions by the road-sides and in the fields. This film was so tangible that we could, with a pointed stick for a pencil, scratch our names in it, names literally " writ in water." The sulphur may have been supplied in part from a number of blast furnaces which were almost constantly in operation in the iron region where these observations were made. I trust the reader's indulgence will be extended to this egotistic episode which is designed to elucidate, in part, the psychic portion of our subject.

XXXIII.

Hypnotism ; Place-Sense of Animals ; Birds and Insects ; Homing Pigeons ; Bees ; Aphides ; Ants ; Keenness of Vision ; Eagle ; Hawk.

It is demonstrated that all the senses are intensified by hypnotism. In those who are subjected to it, the understanding is strengthened, the power of comprehension is enlarged, and that of conception is more acute. They seem to acquire a spiritual prescience that at once reveals to them new objects of cognizance and a wider field of knowledge. Meanwhile, the power of the will over the muscles of the body is suspended as in trances, dreams and visions. But trances, dreams and visions seem to be only varieties or modifications of hypnotism. It must be borne in mind, that hypnotism is the effect induced by natural magnetism in the mind, muscles and nerves of sentient beings. In its eclectic, transcendental character it is, as we have before noted, spiritual, and may be spiritually induced. The action of what is called animal magnetism is manifested in all animal life and, in a little different manner, in all other forms of life.

We have heretofore pointed out the acuteness of vision and of the sense of smell in birds and dogs. But there is another sense or instinct that is more remarkable than either of these. It is the faculty which enables animals, birds and insects to move from place to place in the most direct route that will enable them to reach the object they seek. The males and females of different species of animals living many miles apart, find each other at will, however many angles and turns there may be in the road they may be obliged to follow. If the female desires to see a male, and there are several males living in the neighborhood, but so far apart that she cannot hear the call of either, she will always seek and find the nearest one.

An intelligent shepherd dog, a companion of our youth, liked much in our drives to follow the horses. His master drove one of them to a city thirty-two miles distant. Before starting in the morning, the dog was confined in the coach-house, to remain there until afternoon. He was released about two o'clock, at once took the horse's track, and at six o'clock was with him in the city stable. Two-thirds of the distance he traveled was over a much-used turnpike with many other roads crossing it, and there must have been many equine tracks from which he was to choose.

There is a well-authenticated account of a dog

whose master lived on the Ohio River near Marietta, and during the season boated coal to New Orleans. On one trip he took with him a common shepherd dog, intending to dispose of him. Having sold his boat and cargo, he returned home by steamer, leaving the dog in New Orleans. Some four weeks after, the dog appeared at his master's house, foot-sore, lean, mud-stained and almost famished, after a journey of over 800 miles. Having no track to follow, instinct was his only guide. The homing flight of pigeons and messenger doves, the migratory habits of birds, and the long distances from their nests at which they seek their food, are well known.

But this faculty is still more remarkably exhibited by insects, and most remarkably by the honeybee. Of all communities of organic life the bees are the most wonderful, interesting and edifying to contemplate. Their origin, life, habits, government, sense and sensibility and their acute and accurate *selective* faculty are a marvellous study. The community is composed of three different classes, distinctly differentiated from each other in size, physical structure and functions. There are the drones (males), the largest and least active in motion; then the workers, supposed to be undeveloped females, the smallest in size but the most numerous, most active and efficient, and last the queen, longer in body than the others, more graceful and dignified in her movements, but sufficiently active to lead the others when occasion requires.

In each community or swarm there are from twelve to fifteen thousand workers besides the drones and the queens, and the marvel is that a single queen is the mother of them all. She is also their absolute, infallible ruler, and all her subjects vie with each other in upholding her authority. There are no strikes. The drones are disposed of as soon as the social arrangements for the year are settled, and any objector or obstructor is despatched or exiled without ceremony. Each worker carries in a sheath handy for use his sting, his weapon of defence of himself and of the colony. The queen has the same weapon, but uses it only in self-defence.

At the proper season she deposits from one to two thousand eggs a day. And then is manifested the marvellous selective faculty, the subtle, infallible animal magnetism that enables her to give a specific character to three different classes of eggs. The first and most numerous is the workers, the next the drones, and last the queens. To develop the drones from the egg twenty-five days are necessary, twenty-two for the workers, and sixteen for the queens, and there is no apparent difference between the eggs that produce the three classes. The wonderful *vis-vitæ* of magnetism can alone impart this amazing faculty of selection.

But this faculty is still more surprisingly manifested by the workers. The vision of the bee, so far as we can learn, is quite limited; yet they leave the hive and fly away many miles in all directions in pursuit of flowers, to gather material with which to construct their cells and store them with food. These wonderful cells are correctly constructed on mathematical principles. They are hexagonal in shape, which secures the largest amount of storage room with the least length of side, and no vacant space between. It is also the strongest and safest form of cell since all its sides adjoin and support each other.

We know the uniform color of the honey-comb in each hive and of the honey with which it is filled. But there is a difference in the color of the honey gathered from different flowers. Therefore each bee, through his faculty of selection, works in flowers that yield honey of the same color, and after they return to the hive they show their artistic faculty by blending the different colored honey into one uniform color. They are correct paint mixers, for parti-colored cells are never found in a hive.

Each worker has a little sack for holding honey and a little basket for pollen and bee-glue. When both are filled they rise into the air, and their flight to the hive, however distant it may be, is so direct that the best definition of a straight line is to call it a bee-line. Arriving home the glue and pollen are delivered to the architects for the building of new cells, while the honey is properly prepared and placed in cells already provided.

Now the sovereign ruler of this winged community establishes three of them each year, and does this from three to five years in succession, when old age terminates her career and she is gathered to her mothers. She is not merely the sovereign of these sixty to seventy-five thousand workers with the drones and queens in addition, but she is the mother of every one of them. Consider the intense vitality, the amazing *vis-vitæ* possessed by and stored up in this small insect. Can any lapse of time, any change of conditions evolute her out of her traits, functions and characteristics?

Another remarkable manifestation of the persistence of this same force, this same animal magnetism, is found in the Aphides, the insect that furnishes honey-dew, the favorite food of a certain species of ants. They are especially remarkable for a peculiarity of their generative economy which consists in first fecundation of the female, influencing not only the ova developed immediately afterwards, but those of the females resulting from that development, even to the tenth generation, each of which is successively impregnated and continues to produce without intercourse with the male.

The ants, with whom Sir John Lubbock has so

pleasantly made us familiar, are another remarkable family of insects. Like the bees they live in colonies of thousands in number. Like the bees too, they are divided into three distinct classes, males, females, and neuters, the last being the workers. Some of them also serve as soldiers, carpenters, masons and architects, who plan and build their homes. These are the familiar ant-hills with their numerous galleries, stairways and chambers built on the surface of the ground. Or they may be cavities scooped out under large stones or planks or in decayed, fallen tree trunks. They are phenomenally strong, courageous, industrious and persevering, boldly attacking insects and animals (mice) much larger than themselves. If one of them captures a bug or worm so much larger than himself that he can only move it on a pavement or other similar clear surface, but not through the short grass beside them, he leaves it, goes for help, returns with one or more assistants and the prey is taken home.

We have seen a little brown ant like those so common on side-walks, attack and kill a common caterpillar. The ant climbed on to the neck of the worm, pushed its mandibles through the hair and inserted them in the flesh. The worm was at once alarmed and made desperate efforts to free himself from his enemy by rolling over, curling himself up, and then suddenly snapping himself out, by which means he threw the ant off and then quickened his movements to escape. But the plucky little assailant returned again and again to the attack, always seeking the same spot on the top of the worm's neck. Finally the cuticle was perforated, dark, viscous matter began to ooze out, and death soon followed.

The ants are not only carpenters and masons but they are likewise dairymen and slave-dealers. They have desperate battles, generally lasting two days, in which many on both sides are slain. The victor enslaves his victims and becomes a heartless cannibal. He places his slaves in rows like animals in subterranean stables, where they are fed with the honey-dew which their captors milk and steal from the aphides, above noticed. The poor victims, deluded by the sweet flavor of this food, acquire an inebriate passion for it and gorge themselves until they become puffed up into helpless globular masses, when they are ruthlessly devoured by their cruel conquerors.

The ants communicate with each other through their antennæ as we have witnessed. Passing on the plank·sidewalk of a quiet street we noticed a procession of the little brown ants crossing it diagonally, and stopped to watch their movement. Their home had been, apparently, under the same walk, nearly a block further on. As it had been disturbed by repairs or some other cause, they concluded to seek a new home. It was this migrating procession that we met.

It was about ten rods long, three inches wide, and there must have been thousands of ants in it, marching on in a regular, steady common-time movement.

A number of them had their small white pupa in their mouths. With a little sliver of wood we captured one of these pupa, upsetting the ant to do so. On recovering herself she at once began a search for the pupa. After running anxiously about for some time and not finding it, she stopped several members of the procession who carried no pupa, touched their antennæ with her own and seemed thus to have informed them of her trouble, for they directly joined her in a vigorous search for the lost treasure. Continuing the search until, satisfied that it was fruitless, they reluctantly fell again into the procession. We followed it along by the side of the walk until it reached a point about twelve inches from an oak post of good size that was decayed and hollowed out at the centre. This, it seemed, was to serve for their winter quarters.

Before leaving the birds we wish especially to note the power of vision possessed by the eagle and the hawk. The former after reaching his point look-out descries the small prey he is seeking when several miles distant from it. The hawk from his lofty elevation of two or three thousand feet, sees below the surface of the running water the small fish he wishes to capture. If a black spot the size of this fish were painted on a white board and placed at the same distance from a person with the strongest eyes and most perfect vision he could not see it at all. If we had a refracting telescope whose powers were equal to those of the eagle's eyes, we might be able to distinguish the ships sailing on the seas of Mars if there are any. Perhaps Sir David Brewster's suggestion, that before the end of the century the world will possess a reflecting telescope with a lens twenty feet in diameter, may be realized. If a number of eagle's and hawk's eyes could be obtained and subjected to the most thorough examination that can be made with the improved instruments of the present day, the attainment of this end might be sooner realized.

XXXIV.

Spiders; Their Webs; Ballooning; Securing Prey; Humble-bee and Spider in Death-struggle.

THE spider is not a very attractive or desirable companion and neighbor; on the contrary, he seems nearly as repulsive as the viper tribe, and every man's, and especially every woman's, hand—and broom—are against him. Still, as a form of organic life, he is a very interesting study. Like the ant, he is intelligent, ingenious, courageous and persevering. As spinners and weavers, their work defies competition. The beauty, fineness, evenness and smoothness of their threads are admirable, and the delicacy, thinness, and strength of their silken fabrics are wonderful. They are also architects and artists, and some of them are skilful geometricians, as is shown by their fanciful webs.

The class Tegenaria, who make their parlors near the earth's surface in piles of stone or wood, spread around the parlor door a beautiful and attractive silken carpet which heedless callers find to be most delusively and fatally adhesive. Those callers who enter these parlors must leave hope behind. But the many and sharp-eyed host has sometimes a caller that he fails to secure.

Having, when a boy, been stung by humble-bees and bitten by a spider we were, very naturally, disposed to improve every opportunity to promote the infelicity of both. Fate or chance once gave us an opportunity to bring the two into deadly conflict. Near a famous well from which we often sought a cooling drink was a small pile of cobble-stones. A large, fierce black spider made his spacious parlor and spread the fatal carpet in front near the lower edge of the pile. Near it was a stalk of catnip in blossom. Going to the well for a drink we saw a lusty humble-bee working on the blossoms. With the crown of our straw-hat we gave him a blow that sent him directly on to the silken carpet. He landed on his back with his head towards the parlor door. Instantly the spider darted out and with lightning speed circled round the bee a dozen times or more to bind him fast with his web. When he thought he had the struggling bee sufficiently bound he sprang upon him and seized him by the throat. As they were of the same length the bee curved up his "business end" and thrust his sting into the spider's *other* end. The latter, with greater speed than he had darted out of his parlor, darted back again. So strong were the cords and so skilfully wound that it took the vigorous bee some minutes to disentangle himself and free his wings so that he could use them. He was evidently quite demoralized, for his flight, when he departed, was not normally vigorous. If the spider had seized him in such a way as to have prevented the bee from stinging him he would have been the victor.

We made repeated attempts afterwards, by throwing insects on to the carpet and into the parlor door to induce the occupant to come out. But he never responded. The winds and storms broke the outside fastenings of the carpet, and the establishment fell into decay.

It is well known that some spiders go ballooning and kiting, spinning, for that purpose, a dome-like web and a platform web which may serve as a raft or a sail, with which they make excursions in the air, aided by the wind, and many floating filaments of their silken web.

In his charming work on "American Spiders" Vol. II., Rev. Mr. McCook has fully elucidated the subject of spider ballooning, and described the different methods by which it is accomplished. Not the least interesting portion of his narrative is the description of the manner in which the young spiders in their gossamer ships are distributed in immense numbers over the continents and principal islands of the earth by the trade-winds. Those that are content with less ambitious flights throw out their silver filaments in number and length sufficient to overcome their gravity and sail away in search of a new home. When they wish to alight they have no valves to open, but simply and literally take in their silken sails and quietly settle to the earth.

We were once fortunate enough to witness one of these flittings of a single spider. While trout-fishing down a mountain stream through the woods, we found as we came out into the open that the sun was too pervasive and therefore left the brook where a wood road crossed it and continued on, gradually rising, between a belt of tall trees and an open pasture. While walking next to the pasture fence and looking to the right we saw, against the bright sunlight, a large black wood-spider floating in the air at an elevation of about twenty-five feet, with a thread of her web trailing behind like the tail of a kite and glistening in the sun.

There was a continuous, gentle breeze which did not seem to be sufficiently strong to overcome her gravity. Those who are familiar with New England woods will remember this species of spider: jet black, keen eyes, fierce, repulsive looking and very active in her motions. Her body is covered with long coarse hair and her legs with still coarser, short hair standing nearly at right angles with their length, and presenting a flat appearance like feathers. Possibly the spider had ascended a tall tree standing in the edge of the wood, gone to the outer edge of one of the upper limbs, attached her web to the extreme point, and then swung herself off for a voyage. If her legs were extended side by side and the short, flat-looking hairs interlaced in such a way as to act like feathers and form an aerial raft she would have had sufficient floating capacity. She floated out of sight without any apparent descent in her course.

XXXV.

Lepidoptera; Ova; Larvæ; Cocoon; Chrysalid; Imago; Butterfly; The Cicada; Shell-Life.

ANOTHER remarkable example of the persistence of magnetic *vis-vitæ*, most interesting in form, condition and effect, is presented by the Lepidoptera. The two extremes of this form of life are most marvellous and most intensely interesting, not only in themselves as to what they are, but also as to what they may teach. Let us briefly trace the history of a butterfly.

In the temperate zones from April to November, the eggs are attached to the under-side of the leaves of trees, or other forms of vegetable life, to which they are made fast by a glutinous film that prevents their removal by wind or rain. In the genial warmth of the season development begins at once. With voracious appetites the young grubs devour the tender vegetable fibre, and grow so rapidly that in from five to twenty days the larva attains its full size. These larvæ, caterpillars, of different sizes and colors, as we see them crawling upon the ground or on branches of trees and bushes, are among the lowest and most repulsive creatures that live, and with all persons, except naturalists, they are nearly as unpopular as the viper class. To casual observers their sense and sensibility seem to be exceedingly limited, and they have not a single attractive characteristic. At the proper time the larva seeks, instinctively, a place where it may secrete itself for its grand transformation. And now it begins to manifest its good sense, its reasoning capacity. It desires to protect itself against discovery and attack from its natural enemies and also from the alternations of the weather. Having selected the spot for its temporary burial, its hibernation, it proceeds to construct its own sarcophagus. In doing this it performs the work of an architect and decorator.

The first thing to be done is to build the cocoon, the outer covering of its hibernating domicile. This is cylindrical in form and closed at each end. Its substance is similar to that of a bladder, strong and impervious to air and moisture, and that hardens as it dries. The only tools used by the larva are its legs, spinning apparatus and a supply of raw silk. Having finished the cocoon it next constructs its chrysalid, its coffin. This is a more elaborate piece of work, ovately cylindrical in shape, but largest at the head-end, smooth and polished on its exterior surface, which is punctured by orifices corresponding to its spiracles. The interior is finished off with exquisitely soft and delicate velvet. A more delightful hibernating parlor could not be conceived. The cocoon is also lined with silk velvet, and in due time, when the insect has reached its birth-stage, both are broken open and it escapes.

The period of hibernation varies from six to ten months, but there are some species in which it lasts for two years. This is a most remarkable manifestation of the persistence of animal life, animal magnetism. At the end of the hibernating period the imago appears. Wonderful and beautiful is the Psyche, the winged soul, that comes forth from its sarcophagus, spreads its wings and seeks the skies. In all the range of animal life there is nothing so amazing as the transfiguration and resurrection of the butterfly. Emanating from a minute egg, growing into a repulsive worm with senses and sensibilities of the most limited character, not even having lungs, but breathing through spiracles in its body, possessing no power of rapid motion as it crawls upon the earth, being altogether of the earth, earthy. In this condition, with the aid of a marvellous instinct, it constructs its wonderful tomb, shuts itself up in impenetrable darkness and lies dormant in the hades of departed butterflies from ten to twenty-four months; and then opens the door of its living tomb, emerges into the light of day, expands its beautiful wings, wings which angels might envy if they needed them, wings resplendent in most exquisite colors that might have been born of the sunshine of Paradise; it waves these and flies away over the earth, drawing new life from its atmosphere and nursing on the dewy nectar of its flowers, a flying orchid, living on dew and air.

NOTE—In the museum of Cornell University there is a large and fine collection of butterflies. Many of them are exceedingly beautiful.

And what is the lesson to be learned from this wondrous life? First, it is an irrefragable proof of the resurrection of a body, not indeed from death, but from a comatose state near akin to it, the same but different, identical but transfigured. Every particle of matter that entered into the chrysalid came out of it. Every particle that went into it was a living particle; every particle that came out of it was also a living particle. There was no stain nor lifeless particle left within the velvet chamber. Second, it is an equally irrefragable proof of the persistence, the constant pervasive energy, the *vis-viva* of the magnetic force in animal life and in varying phases of it. It begins with the egg, it continues in the larva, it survives the long night of years in the chrysalid, and develops into perfect life in the beautiful imago, the perfect butterfly.

There is no friction, no impact, no induction, no possible method of developing electric action in this system. It is animal magnetism pure and simple.

But the most persistent living force and the most protracted period of hibernation are exhibited by the cicada-septemdecim. He buries himself at an unknown depth in the ground and only appears again on its surface after a lapse of seventeen years.

Another most interesting form of life is shell life, ranging in age and size from the gigantic conch down to the families of the infinitesimal Limaconidæ, Tripteridæ, Truncatellas, and Lonites. As a general rule their cradles are their graves, their homes are their tombs. These are constructed of pearl, marble, and limestone. The architecture of many of them in structure, form, color and ornamentation is exquisitely beautiful, and admirably adapted to the comfort and safety of their occupants. They abound, live and thrive on the land and in both salt and fresh water. The iridescent decoration of the parlor of the pearl is indescribably beautiful, while the exterior ornamentation of many of them is hardly less attractive. On the other hand, the houses of the oyster are very rough and uninviting. They are the log cabins of concological architecture. The taste of the occupants however, is unimpeachable.

XXXVI.

Animal Instincts; Selective Faculty.

THERE is another remarkable faculty or instinct exhibited by some animals scarcely noticed hitherto. It is the selective faculty that prompts them to refrain from eating poisonous, or, for them, unhealthy food, and to do certain things necessary for the safety and comfort of their offspring.

Kine avoid all poisonous plants if they stand isolated in the field, but they sometimes unconsciously eat cow-bane—cicuta—which may be concealed in a cluster of other nutritious and innocuous plants. Cattle ranging in pastures, however hungry, will not touch the foliage of spotted alder, poison sumach, poison ivy, nor any other poisonous shrubs. Cows in wild pastures with their newborn calves when they wish to range for their food seek a secluded shade where they compel the calf to lie down and make it understand that it must not move until the cow return. While feeding she keeps vigilant watch in the direction of its hiding place to see that it is not disturbed. We knew a fine cow that dropped her calf in such a pasture, hid it, ranged off to feed, was taken ill and died. Some days after the calf was found half starved, where she had concealed it, and taken home.

The traveller on the western prairies fifty years ago would occasionally notice, as we have done, certain circular and semicircular paths about ten feet in diameter. They were made by mother buffaloes caught out on the prairie in bleak, cold wind and rainstorms. If the wind was strong and fixed in one direction, the mother made the calf lie down on the lee side of such slight elevation as she could find. Then she walked back and forth in a semicircle between the calf and the wind for the double purpose of breaking the force of the wind and permitting the warmth from her body to be wafted over the calf. Occasionally she laid down with her back to the wind and adjusted her body and legs in a way to inclose the calf. She kept this position until she became chilly, getting rest in the meantime. If the wind was of the character of a whirlwind coming from different quarters, she walked in a circle around the calf, alternating as before with the lying down.

It is a difficult thing for the most expert naturalist to catch a fly in his hand. We have seen a garden toad leap sixteen or eighteen inches and catch one from a board fence. But we have not succeeded, after repeated trials, in inducing a toad to devour a potato beetle or a squash bug.

People can learn much out-of-doors if they only *see* what they *look at* and endeavor to understand its significance, its function. During a three weeks stay at the Chicago Fair, according to our observation, not one person in 10,000 *saw* the beautiful decorations in the domes of the entrances to all except the matchless recessed arch of the Transportation Building. In the daily throngs entering we did not see a single person looking up at them except the few who stopped to see what we were gazing at.

XXXVII.

Spiritual Force. Mental Force. Magnetic Power Greater in Small than in Large Magnets.

There is another remarkable and subtle force to which we have slightly alluded in treating of persons designated as magnetic, which varies materially from the descriptive detail of the action of that force. It is a spiritual, mental force. This different manifestation of force is best summarized by St. Paul : "Now there are diversities of gifts but the same spirit.* * *   For to one is given by the spirit the word of wisdom ; to another the word of knowledge by the same spirit ; to another faith by the same spirit; to another the gift of healing by the same spirit ; to another the working of miracles ; to another prophecy ; to another discovering of spirits; to another divers kinds of tongues ; to another the interpretation of tongues : But all these worketh that one and the self-same spirit, dividing to every man as he will."*

All experience confirms this diversity of gifts and demonstrates that no one individual possesses

---
I. Corinthians, chap. 12, v. 4 *et seq.*

them all, though some may possess more than others. All persons are differentiated from each other by difference of gifts. There are, so to speak, many similars, no identicals. Some are mathematicians, some philosophers, some poets, some musicians, some painters, some sculptors, some architects, some inventors, and some with no power of mental concentration in any direction.

These differences are shown in divers ways in the ordinary affairs of life. Some men are genial, generous, active, willing to live and let live. They seem to be favorites of fortune, and everything they touch turns to gold. Others, with the same equipment as to age, strength, ability and willingness to work, may yet delve a lifetime and barely live. Some have great executive ability who, with few adventitious aids, but with indomitable courage and resolution successfully accomplish a vast amount of work, both mental and physical. Others with equal mental capacity have no executive ability, are infirm of purpose, sporadic, miscellaneous, and, although fairly industrious, accomplish but little.

Notice half-a-dozen well-grown boys sitting side by side and fishing from the flume in a dam or from the bank of a stream. One or two are more or less successful, at short intervals catching a fish. The others do not succeed. They drop their lines as near as possible to those of the fortunates; they exchange tackle with them. All in vain, they catch no fish. These unfortunates, when they " go a-fishing" do so with the hope that they may succeed; rather doubtful, but they will try.

The fortunates go, not only with the hope, but with the determination, to catch fish. They are in earnest. They add to their hope faith, and so an effluence of trust and confidence pervades their work: and their faith and hope are justified by their work, the fish are caught. We often hear it remarked that people fail in this or that undertaking because they are only "half-hearted" in their work, they put no energy, resolution into it. This is true, and it is only another way of saying that they are weak in magnetic power, which is will-power.

In all forms of life the life-force, the animal magnetism, is a dyad and life is perpetuated by a force that has two poles. In diœcious forms procreation is effected by copulation of the sexes; in monœcious forms the two poles are adjacent as in the minute, almost infinitesimal atoms of the lodestone.

Reproduction commences in the acephala—oysters—long before full growth is obtained. The cyclas—sphærium—reproduces when so immature as to possess hardly any of the external characters of the species; and oysters, although they do not attain full growth under three or four years, yet spawn when they are four months old. So prolific are they that the ova of a single oyster have been estimated as high as ten millions in number.

The almost infinite variety in the forms of life

is as astonishing as its wonderful persistence, and the infinite divisibility of matter is paralleled by the infinite divisibility of the *vis-vitæ*. Considering the exhibition of magnetic power in all forms of animal life, it is interesting to note the fact that small magnets are much stronger in proportion to their size than larger ones, and that the pressure is greater on the surface of small planets than on those of greater ones in proportion to their mass.* If the magnetic power of the whale were proportionally larger than that of the honey-bee he might carry ships on his back, and if the magnetic power of the elephant were proportionally greater than that of the little brown ant, he might pull up trees to get his lunch instead of breaking off their branches.

* Sir Isaac Newton's 18th Query.

XXXVIII.

Force and Matter.—Some Suggestions Concerning their Indestructibility, and Variety of Forms.

WE have already referred to the extraordinary power exhibited in the physical mechanism of man and other animals when under cataleptic, hypnotic and other abnormal influences and especially noted the fact that the power, the force thus developed is *brain* power, or force, *will* force. "An arm, the muscles of which are lamed, is incapable of doing any work; the moving force of the muscles must be at work in it and these must obey the nerves which bring to them orders from the *brain*. That member is then capable of the greatest variety of motions; it can compel the most varied instruments to execute the most diverse tasks." * The fact, the existence, the necessity of Force is a grand, fundamental truth underlying all the phenomena of life and nature. We can make no progress in any department of natural science without the aid of some kind of force.

"Force and matter," says Mayer, "are indestruc-

* Helmholtz, Pop. Sci. Lect., p. 321.

tible objects. Force is something which is expended in producing motion. Two classes of causes occur in nature, which so far as experience goes, never pass one into another. The first class consists of such causes as possess the properties of weight and impenetrability: the other class is made up of causes which are wanting in the properties just mentioned " which are called also imponderables."

"Nature," says Helmholtz, "as a whole possesses a store of force which cannot in any way be increased or diminished. * * * Therefore the quantity of force in nature is just as eternal and unalterable as the quantity of matter. According to this we can divide the total force-store of the universe into two parts, one of which is heat and must continue as such; the other to which a portion of the heat of the warmer bodies and the total supply of chemical, electrical and magnetical forces belong, is capable of the most varied changes of form and constitutes the whole wealth of change which takes place in nature."*

"No force," says Grove, † "can be, strictly speaking, initial, as there must be some anterior force which produced it. We cannot create force or motion any more than we can create matter. Can we, indeed, suggest a proposition definitely conceivable by the mind, of force without ante-

---
* Helmholtz, Pop. Sci. Lec., pp. 171-2.
† Correlation of Phys. Forces, pp. 195-6.

cedent force? "I cannot without calling for the interposition of created power. * * * The impossibility, humanly speaking, of creating or annihilating matter has long been admitted. The reasons for the admission of a similar doctrine as to force appear to be equally strong."

"With regard to matter there are many causes in which we never (can) practically prove the cessation of its existence, yet we do not the less believe in it; who, for instance, can trace so as to reweigh the particles of iron worn off from a carriage wheel? or re-combine the particles of wax dissipated and chemically changed in the burning of a candle?"

"Considering the continued activity of the sun through countless centuries we may assume, with mathematical certainty, the existence of some compensating influence to make good its enormous loss. By a law which is universally true, waste and want go hand in hand. Laplace demonstrated that the length of the day remained constant for 2,500 years." *

From Geology we learn that the temperature of the earth has remained practically the same for hundreds of thousands of years, and hence it follows that the same is true of the temperature of the sun. Hence again it follows that some cause of the constant supply of the sun's heat other than that of the contraction of its mass must be sought,

* Mayer, Cel. Dyn., pp. 265, 326.

since there is no evidence of the diminution of its diameter. It is demonstrated that but a small portion of the heat emanating from the sun is distributed to the planets in the solar system. Hence arises the "enormous loss" to which Mayer refers as having been sustained by it "through countless centuries."

Where shall we seek the "compensating influence to make good this enormous loss" and so preserve the equilibrium of the solar system? By our hypothesis, as before noted, an inexhaustible supply of fuel is furnished from the *outer* stellar space, not only for our sun but for all the suns in the omniverse. This supply is ample, immanent, constant and is immediately furnished wherever "waste," "loss," exhaustion or dissipation of matter has occurred, thus maintaining the equilibrium of every system.

XXXIX.

Number and Duration of Suns and Planets.

We have noted the popular idea that the stars are infinite in number and duration. Treating of the stellar distances Father Secchi* says: "Immense as this space may seem it does not constitute the real limit of the creation, since our most powerful instruments fail to penetrate even all the galactic strata in all their profundity; hence the firmament for us is unfathomable. Nevertheless it cannot be called infinite; nothing composed of distinct and separate entities can be called infinite. It is said that the world ought to be infinite, in order that the work may be worthy of its infinite Creator. But if it were infinite and peopled to infinity with stars, the celestial vault ought to appear, in all its extent, as brilliant as the sun. Such is not the fact, and hence we must conclude that the stars are not infinite in number."

This argument is conclusive.

The conditions of our new Cosmography help us to comprehend, to a reasonable extent, what

* Johnson's Cyclopedia, Art., "Universe."

has hitherto been considered incomprehensible. In that system all the celestial bodies are formed within the hyperboloids and the asymptoid which together constitute the omniverse. The divine, transcendent light proceeding from the centre of the asymptoid, enveloping and passing beyond the supernal spheres within it, will gradually diminish in intrinsic brightness as it recedes from that centre. In like manner, the solar rays, emanating from all the suns in all the hyperboloids and reflected from all planets, will also gradually fade out as they recede from the same centre until finally the whole omniverse will be enveloped in the utter darkness of outer space, thus presenting the appearance, from any point from which it could be visible, of a vast globe of mild radiance, flecked, as it were, with numerous shadows on a field totally dark. And although this omniverse is constantly increasing in size, we can comprehend its limits so far as to understand that it can never fill all space, and consequently that it can never contain an infinite number of celestial bodies.

We have shown that the calorific rays of the sun after leaving its atmosphere are totally dark, and that they do not become luminous until they encounter some opaque or resisting medium by which they are reflected and refracted. This is conclusively proved by the fact that if the opaque body be of any considerable magnitude, like a planet, the side opposite the sun is totally dark, and if the planet did not revolve on its axis, so that every part of its surface could be subjected, at short intervals, to the luminous rays, it would become intensely cold and perfectly desolate. On the contrary, if the hemisphere exposed to the direct rays of the sun were so exposed for any considerable period of time the heat concentrated upon it would be so intense that its waters, its moisture, would be entirely evaporated and all forms of life would perish. The moon is a sublime object-lesson that partially illustrates this condition of things.

There is one supreme truth that we are compelled to recognize, that namely, that all *life* is the result of a *force*. Another cardinal fact is that no force can be made manifest except through the instrumentality of matter.

Magnetism requires the lodestone, a metal, the air or a fluid or a gas to make its presence known. Electricity requires the proper machine, the inductive cylinders or coils, the amber, the wax, the clouds and moisture or a peculiar condition of the atmosphere for its development. The mental powers, the mind, the thought, the will, can only manifest themselves through brain and muscle and nerves. Equally true it is that there can be no life without the aid of heat and moisture; also that there can be no life in the extremes of heat and cold, in other words, that there are degrees of temperature, calorific and frigorific, beyond which life cannot be sustained.

We know that there can be no vegetable life without light. In the mammoth cave of Kentucky and in all caves where total and constant darkness prevails, there is no least manifestation of vegetable or plant life.

But light is not necessary for the development of animal life, as is abundantly demonstrated by the blind fish in the mammoth cave and the forms of life in the extreme depths of the ocean, as well as beneath the surface of the earth.

Since matter and force are held to be indestructible, and since force can be made manifest only through matter, it must follow that every organism, animal, plant or vegetable, is a mechanical structure operated by *some* force. But these organisms are endowed with a force that enables them to perpetuate themselves indefinitely, each after its kind. Hence that force must be constant, pervasive, effective. As we have repeatedly noted, there is in nature but *one* force that invariably and perfectly fulfills these conditions, that is, the magnetic force. Hence, if there be no error in our facts and no fault in our reasoning, the inexorable logic of the concept is that there can be no life without magnetism. And especially noticeable is the marvellous adaptability of this force to every organism, however immense or minute. The working of the brain of the little brown ant is as perfect and wonderful as that of man or the elephant, of the humming-bird as that of the condor.

XL.

Conclusion.

WITH the exception of some experiments designed to demonstrate the correctness of some of our most important propositions, but which we have not been able to secure the facilities for performing, our task is finished. Probably no student in astronomy or physics ever laid down his textbooks without feeling that some of the most important conclusions arrived at were not conclusive, that there was a hiatus, a something wanting that ought to be attained in order that our reason should be satisfied. He feels that he is very near the grand goal of truth, but has not quite reached it; that, Moses like, he has had a charming view of the fair fields of the celestial Canaan, but still has not been permitted to wander through them nor to taste their grapes nor drink their wine.

All the problems connected with our own solar system are so thoroughly elucidated that when we have mastered them we commence our explorations in the boundless areas of space with a cheerful hope and strong faith that the sublimest results will be soon attained.

We get into the Milky Way. It is an enchanting way to follow. New beauties and glories, aspects more and more sublime, are revealed at every step. But it returns into itself and we end where we began. We find that our stellar system is but a small part of this illuminated way, and that its primary—the sun—is only a brilliant point lost in a galaxy of other points far larger and more brilliant.

Vast as is the extent of this galaxy, yet how small a portion of the firmament does it fill! Concerning the Galactic Circle Sir John Herschel[1] writes: "It is to sidereal what the invariable ecliptic is to planetary astronomy—a plane of ultimate reference, the ground plan of the sidereal system." It may be compared to the cross-section of an immense cylinder, populated with stars, in some parts so densely that the highest telescopic power of vision does not enable us to sound their utmost depths; in other parts so sparsely that we look through them into "coal sac's" of impenetrable darkness.

Looking north and south, so to speak, from the centre of this cylinder, we observe numerous groups of stellar matter twinkling and moving apparently in all directions, direct and retrograde, angular and oblique, with little or no system or order, like swarms of insects in a summer sky.

From a careful review of the various facts and

[1] Outlines of Astronomy, p. 450.

conclusions which we have presented it seems certain that the Galaxy is the grandest feature, the sublimest outgrowth of the stellar geography, the celestial cosmography; that it forms a zone or group of stellar systems which occupies one of the hyperboloids; the most perfect and the most brilliant of these systems being nearest to the hyperboloidal centre, while those which are less perfect, less complete, lie further from that centre; the nebulæ and nubuculæ lying still more remote, being the last and most minute forms of matter which occupy the border-land of the hyperboloidal space. The planets that are nearest their primaries are the oldest, and the north or positive pole of each stellar system points toward the grand, common centre of them all.

The centres and motions of individual solar systems are well understood, but all effort to establish a common centre for all stellar systems has, thus far, failed. As the reader will have observed, our principal object has been to establish that centre and to show how all possible stellar systems with all possible forces and motions are inexorably connected with it.

In developing our hypothesis we have, with an iteration and reiteration that may seem wearisome but that we have deemed essential, set forth, specialized and emphasized the properties and characteristics of one particular force, namely, magnetism. And in order to demonstrate more fully its manifold virtues, offices and functions, we have ranged into the department of psychology. If the nature of this force in its normal and transcendental functions as herein unfolded and interpreted, shall, by the use of more perfect instruments and further observation be proved and accepted as true, then we have a reasonable solution of all psychological and physical problems.

If it be asked why we have selected the asymptoid, the hyperboloids and the hyperbola for the outlines of our celestial geography and the forms of space in which all matter can exist and all the natural and certain supernatural forces can be manifested, the reply is, because they are best adapted to accomplish the end proposed and that they possess peculiar properties and characteristics that are possible in no other forms.

And while it is true that innumerable hyperbolas can be cut from cones whose sides make any angle at their vertices from zero to 90°, yet it is also true that the hyperbola cut from what we have called a right angle cone is the only one that can fulfil the conditions of our hypothesis.

The hyperboloid that revolves about its transverse axis generates a hyperboloid of two nappes. These are surfaces of double curvature; they are conjugate, symmetrical, homogeneous, homologous and their equations are identical. If two conjugate hyperbolas are revolved about either axis they will generate a pair of conjugate hyperboloids of revolution and their common asymptotes will generate a cone which separates the two. There are no other curves known that can possibly fulfil these conditions. How admirably and perfectly they are fitted for the construction of our new cosmography must be at once apparent. There are no hidden angles or corners connected with them. Perfectly, systematically, harmoniously they occupy all space. All forms of matter, all forms of energy, all processes of life and growth, all processes of decay and death, exist and are manifested within them.

Finally we wish further to emphasize the fact that the supreme origin, centre, source, germ and root of the new System is DEITY. All spirit, power, energy, force; all life, matter, motion are the direct outcome of His will, the result of His laws. Ample material, ample ways and means are provided for the execution of those laws, with endless space and time for their perpetual development. And thus the grand processes of nature are forever carried forward, and thus with ever-increasing reason, ever-growing emphasis, the firmament showeth forth the handiwork and the heavens declare the glory of GOD.

Such is the system which, with due humility but with an abiding faith in its substantial verity, is submitted for the consideration of investigators, and with some appropriate words from Grove we submit it to their criticism : " That the theoretical portions of this essay are open to objections I am fully conscious. I cannot, however, but think that the fair way to test a theory is to compare it with other theories, and to see whether, upon the whole, the balance of probability is in its favor. Were a theory open to no objections it would cease to be a theory and become a law; and were we not to theorize or to take generalized views of natural phenomena until those generalizations were sure and unobjectionable—in other words were laws—science would be lost in a complex mass of unconnected observations, which would probably never disentangle themselves."

THE END.

INDEX.

A.
Abbott, Mrs., 105 *et seq.*
Aerial Music, 217.
Age of Earth, 158 *et seq.*
Age of the Stars, 164 *et seq.*
Addison, 171, Note.
Aqueous Vapor, 150, 76.
Alpha Centauri, 195.
Ampère, 26.
Ammonia, 184.
Anaxagoras, 58.
Andrews, 41.
Ångström, 55.
Animal Magnetism, 197 *et seq.*, 233 *et seq.*, 239.
Animals, 239, 259.
Answered Prayer, 183.
Ants, 239 *et seq.*, 246.
Arago, 25.
Aphides, 239.
Attributes of God, 64.
Asymptoid, 173, 178, 181, 185.
Aurora, 96.
Apostles, 227.

B.
Bacon, 11, 215.
Bain, 121, 124.
Barnard, President, 195, Note.
Beginnings, 64, 72.
Bancalari, 134.
Bees, 239, *et seq.*
Bernheim, 198.
Birds, 239 *et seq.*
Brain, 110 *et seq.*, 199, 200, 208.
Browne, Sir Thomas, 68.
Burke, E., 81.
Butterflies, 254 *et seq.*

C.
Capella, Light of, 196.
Cat, 80, 234.
Carbon, 136.
Center of all Space, 192.
Celestial Geography, 140 *et seq.*, 169.
Caterpillars, 250.
Chemical Force, 27, 28, 34, 198.
Chrysalid, 254.
Cocoon, 254.
Chapman, 130.
Carnot, 25.
Cicada, 58.
Clark, Dr., 65.
Conductors, 126.
Coulomb, 73, 82.
Cook, 136.
Cosmography, The new, 22', 169.
Color, 28, 78, 89, 35, 139.
Comets, 54, 145.
Condor, 82.
Conarium, 116.
Charcot, 198.
Combustion, 152.
Currents, Afferent and Efferent, 126.
Creation, 61, 62.
Crookes, 40.

D.
Darwin, 29.
Daniell, 27.
Davy, Sir H., 49, 89.
Diamonds, 137.
Delirium Tremens, 197.
Devotion, 197.
Democritus, 58.
Dewar, 107.
Diastole and Sistole, 128.
Dogs, 80, 234.
Draper, J. W., 49.
Dreams, 209 *et seq.*
Dust of Time, 145.
Descartes, 119.

E.
Eagle, 81, 83, 247.

INDEX.

Earth, Age of, 158 *et seq*.
Effluence, 66, 68, 74.
Electricity, 36, 89, 92, 199.
Electricity of Plants, 203, 204.
Emerson, R. W., 68.
Electro-Chemic Force, 28.
Epicurus, 59.
Energy, 86, 91.
Ether, 153, 187.
Exhilarating Atmosphere, 185, 186.
Evolution, 67, 187.
Experiments in Magnetism, 43.

F.

Faraday, 22 *et seq*., 88, 90, 91, 134, 139.
Fibres, 111, 115, 126, 80.
Ferrier, 110, 125-6, 131, 207.
Firefly, 18, 139.
Flame, 150.
Flowers, 204.
Force, Disruptive, 94, 86, 91, 266.

G.

Gases, 132 *et seq*., 183.
Gauss, 24.
Gassiot, 37, 41.
Ganot, 49.
Geisler's Tubes, 36.
Gravity, 49, 53.
Geography, Celestial, 140.
Graining of Wood, 28, 30.
Grey, 34.
Grove, 19, 41, 49.
Glow-worm, 182.
Gould, 167.
God, Attributes, 64.
God, Dwelling Place, 179.
God, 57, 68, 190, *et seq*.
Gland, Pineal, 115 *et seq*.
Glashier, 46.

H.

Harris, 94.
Hawks, 81, 93.
Hansteen, 167.

Heart, 127 *et seq*., 247.
Herschel, Sir Wm., 143, 166.
Herschel, Sir John, 54.
Heat, 88, 89, 91.
Heat, Radiant, 36.
Hegel, 70, 71.
Hertz, Experiments, 93, 102.
Heredity, 202.
Helmholtz, 18, 26, 63, 88, 267.
Hair, 233 *et seq*.
Hodge, 92.
Horse, 83-4, 201.
Hopkinson, 36, 40, 50.
Holmes, Dr. O. W., 65, 66.
Humble-bees, 249.
Humboldt, 84, 167-8.
Hydrogen, 76, 135.
Hyperboloids, 173, 175.
Hypnotism, 239 *et seq*.
Huggins, Dr., 147, 155.

I.

Imago, 257.
Instinct, 72, 259.
Insects, 72, 239.

J.

James, Prof., 125.
Jesus, 65, 68.
Joule, 39.

K.

Kant, 11, 42, 60, 67.
Kirschoff, 55.
Kolrauch, 55.

L.

Laughing Gas, 136.
Laër, 80.
Lambert, 141.
Ladd, 121, 126.
Langley, 139, 148.
Larvæ, 254.
Leibnitz, 42, 51.
Lambert, 141.
Leucippus, 58.
Light, 92, 97 *et seq*.
Lepidoptera, 254 *et seq*.
Light without Heat, 182.

Lucretius, 59.
Lockyear, 148.
Lodge, Dr., 187.
Love, 201.
Life Changes, 194.
Lodestone, 47, 78-9, 150.
Lotze, 69.
Lost Articles Returned, 229 et seq.

M.

Magnetism, Compressible, 36, 38, 90.
Magnetism, Animal, 105 et seq., 197.
Magnetism, Transcendental, 57, 70.
Magnetism, 24, 43, 47, 90, 198.
Magnetism, 22 et seq.
Magnets, Power of Large and Small, 262.
Magnetic Poles, 168.
Magnetic Men and Women, 200.
Matter, 10, 64, 68, 180 et seq.
Matter, Transcendental, 180 et seq.
Marcus Aurelius, 10.
Martyrs, 201.
Magnesphere, 193.
Magellanic Clouds, 155, 156.
Milky Way, 60, 62, 273.
Mental Conversation, 215.
Mental Questions and Answers, 215.
Mind Reading, 215.
Maxwell, 17, 91.
Magendie, 121.
Mayer, 86, 87.
Music, Piano and Harp, 218.
Music, Piano Beating Time, 215.
Motion, 19, 74, Rotary, 63, 64.
Muscular Action, 198
Müller, 28.

N.

Nappes, 170, 174.
Natural Forces, 267.
Nebulæ, 141, 143.
Nebular Conglomeration, 63.
Nerves, 124, 126, 128.
Newton, Sir Isaac, 52, 67, 73.
Newcomb, Prof., 6, 141.
Nitrogen, 135, 184, 185.
Nordenskjold, 146.

O.

Ocular Spectrum, 235.
Odors, 81.
Oersted, 26.
Omniverse, 193, 271.
Ova, 254.
Oxygen, 76, 80, 91, 137.

P.

Pain, 128.
Perpetual Motion, 177, 189.
Pineal Gland, 116 et seq.
Physical and Psychic Force, 198.
Pigeons, 241.
Piano, Beating Time, 219.
Place-sense of Animals, 240 et seq.
Plants, 28, 78-9.
Planchette, 221.
Planetary Systems, 13.
Planets and Spheres, Life in them, 193.
Plücker, 50.
Poles, Magnetic, 168.
Personal Experience, 233.
Prayer Answered, 183.
Procreation, 201.
Prenatal Impressions, 202.
Presentiment, 209.
Preëxperience, 207, 209.
Primordial Matter, 65.

Q.

Quain, 115, 121.

R.

Radiant Heat, 40, 181.

Radiant Light, 184.
Radiant Matter, 40, 186.
Raven, 81.
Ribot, 198.
Reminiscence, 197.
Reappearance of Lost Articles, 229 *et seq*.
Reason, 72, 81.
Rheotem.
Ross, Sir James, 167.
Rotary Motion, 63-4.

S.

Sachs, 32.
Saviour, 68.
Secchi, Father, 142, 164, 173, 194, 270.
Selective Faculty, 259.
Sinews, 124.
Sirius, Light of, 195.
Schelling, 149.
Solar Light, 55.
Seeds, 203, 205.
Soul, 112.
Southern Hemisphere, 166 *et seq*.
Smell, Sense of, 80, 84, 240.
Spectrum of Gas Flame, 149 *et seq*.
Spiritual Transformations, 194.
Spiritual Force, 262.
Semi-spiritual Substance, 64.
Spirit, 71, 187, 223, 262.
Space, Centre of all, 192.
Space, Extra Stellar, 73, 189.
Spiders, 249, *et seq*.
Solar Systems, 188.
Space, 9, 13, 178.
Spiritism, 187, Systematic Investigation, 215.
Subtle Force, 229.
Shell Life, 258.
Stellar Distances, 270.
Stellar Systems, 13, 72, 140 *et seq*., 189.

Stars, 60, 156-7, Star-dust, 173, 176.
Spheres, Celestial, Life in them, 194.
Swedenborg, 59, 67, 167.
Sun, 161.

T.

Telepathy, 183.
Tesla, 182.
Tait, 26.
Time, 9.
Thomson, Sir William, 18, 36.
Thalen, 55.
Thrills, 233, 236.
Thought Transference, 215.
Tissues, 200.
Touch, Sense of, 83-4.
Trance, Speaking and Writing, 215.
Tides, 54.
Trees, 29.

U.

Universal Force, 36.
Universe, 70, 30, 32.
Universes, 193.

V.

Vacua, 36 *et seq*., 53.
Vision, 235, 239, 240, 247.

W.

Water, 138.
Wartman, 203.
Winchell, Prof. Alexander, 63, 145, 147.
Winslow, 114.
World Systems, 57, 61, 74.
World-stuff, 64, 71, 72.
Wright, T. F., 59.

Y.

Young, Dr. Thomas, 49.

Z.

Zantedeshi, 134.

www.ingramcontent.com/pod-product-compliance
Lightning Source LLC
Chambersburg PA
CBHW032101230426
43672CB00009B/1601